Total
stress
Relief

Other books by Vera Peiffer

Positive Living (Piatkus)
Inner Happiness (Piatkus)
Positive Thinking
More Positive Thinking
Positively Fearless
Positively Single
How to Cope with Splitting Up
How to Say No

VERA PEIFFER

Total stress *Relief*

practical solutions THAT really work

PIATKUS

First published in 2003 by
Judy Piatkus (Publishers) Limited
5 Windmill Street
London W1T 2JA
e-mail: info@piatkus.co.uk

The moral right of the author has been asserted

A catalogue record for this book is available from the British Library

ISBN 0 7499 2423 3

Edited by Lizzie Hutchins

This book has been printed on paper manufactured with respect for the
environment using wood from managed sustainable resources

Typeset by Action Publishing Technology, Gloucester
Printed & bound in Great Britain by
Butler & Tanner Ltd, Frome, Somerset

For my friend
Max Delli Guanti
Thank you for holding the vision for both of us.

A diamond is a lump of charcoal that made good under pressure.

Contents

Introduction   1

PART ONE **Stress Signals**

1. **Recognising stress**   9
   SOS signals   13
   Stress resilience   25
   Are you a stress-prone personality?   27

PART TWO **Stress Busting**

2. **Assessing your stress levels**   35
   What is your stress quotient?   37

3. **Strengthening mental resilience**   43
   Mental quick fixes   44
   Practical exercises   45
     Short meditation   45
     Short meditation   45
     Stop overthinking   46
     Give your brain an oxygen hit   47
     The Crown Pull   47
     Self-hypnosis   48
     The Screen Exercise   49
     Anticipating success   50
   Mental self-sabotage   51
     Drugs and alcohol   51
     Letting your mind run away with you   55

Food for thought 57
  Are you a square peg in a round hole? 57
  Giving a clear 'no' message 61
  Staying positive 62
  Managing your time effectively 65

4. **Coping with emotional upheaval** 68
Emotional quick fixes 69
Practical exercises 70
  The Overload Soother 70
  Under-8-Breathing 70
  The Stress Tap 72
  The Pyramid of Peace 74
  The Respect Exercise 77
  A protective shield 80
Emotional self-sabotage 81
  Blaming and generalising 82
  Putting up with the unbearable 84
Food for thought 87
  Relationships: shockers or shock absorbers? 87
  Boundaries and rules 91
  Using anger constructively 95
  Contagious moods 99
  Dealing with difficult people 101
  Are you an energy vampyr? 105

5. **Supporting the body** 108
Physical quick fixes 109
Practical exercises and tips 110
  Wake-up Call exercises 110
  Belly breathing 111
  Acupressure and reflexology 113
  Yoga 115

Snacks that help you sleep 118
Physical self-sabotage 119
Smoking 119
Neglecting your life rhythm 121
Sugar – destruction from within 124
Stress and dehydration 127
Food for thought 129
How healthy are dairy products? 129
Why we need supplements 132
Mercury and Stress 134

6. The holistic first aid kit 138
Vitamins, minerals and amino acids 140
Healing herbs 148
Flower remedies 151
Aromatherapy oils 154
Help for exhausted glands 159

Further Reading 163
Useful Addresses 166
Index 175

Introduction

You probably think that you have no time to read this book because you are too stressed. To tell you the truth, I thought *I* was too stressed to *write* this book, but I did it anyway and found it very useful to remind myself of all the excellent easy-to-learn and quick-to-use methods there are to help you cope with stress and even thrive on it! So if I could manage to *write* this book, you won't have any problems *reading* it. Just do it slowly. Read one section at a time and do the exercises, and you will gradually notice that you are regaining more and more control of your life, recouping lost energy and beginning to enjoy yourself again.

Total Stress Relief is easy to read and clearly laid out. You will find concise descriptions of how stress develops and how it affects body, mind and behaviour. The exercises are simple and effective, and most of them only take a few minutes to do. That means that these stress busters will not add to your stress by taking up even more of your time!

These powerful techniques derived from cognitive psychology, positive thinking, hypnotherapy and reflexology are designed to help you quickly and effectively regain control of your life, your time and your sanity. The book also includes exercises which work on a physical, mental and emotional level, and nutritional tips and advice on selecting the right supplements for you.

The most natural response to stress is to try and avoid it. If your boss is giving you grief on a daily basis, the most liberating thing would be to just walk out of the office and never return. If you are struggling with being single, you could latch on to the nearest person who is willing to go out with you, just to get away from your feelings of loneliness. If you feel overwhelmed by the responsibilities of holding down a job and looking after a family, you could start popping pills to keep you going. But none of this would solve your problems.

Avoiding stress is not an option. It doesn't work. If you run away from stress, it will run after you, and it can run faster than you! It makes much more sense to face your stress, evaluate it and then take positive action. The more skilled you become at dealing with pressures and demands, the greater the stress resilience you develop. Avoiding stress makes you weak because you are not making use of your mental, emotional and physical coping abilities. Like a muscle that is underused, your stress resilience starts to dwindle when you avoid dealing with life's pressures. A flabby muscle is no good in an emergency when you need to lift something heavy; a toned muscle can cope.

Not knowing how to deal with stress perpetuates the problem. If you feel helpless or angry whenever a particular situation occurs, you will become fearful of the same thing happening again. When you are being overburdened with work by your boss and you don't tackle this problem in one way or another, you are bound to dread the next working day. You take your exhaustion and frustration home with you, don't sleep very well as a consequence and then go in the next day tired and demoralised. Not a good start to a day that holds mountains of work for you!

Stress management is more than just damage limitation when life gets bumpy – it is part of your personal development. Remember back to maybe 10 or 20 years ago when you were less experienced in so many aspects of life – everything took you twice as long to do as it does now. You were thrown by things that wouldn't make you bat an eyelid today. You were nervous about tackling issues that now are only a minor blip in your daily routine. We may not like adversity, but it can make us a lot stronger, add to our inner resources and make us feel in charge of our lives, *if we know how to overcome it*. This is what *Total Stress Relief* is all about. It doesn't matter how hopeless or stressful a situation appears, there is *always* a way forward.

If you want to become stronger, more resourceful and take back control of your life, read this book from cover to cover. Read it in your own time, start using the exercises and watch your progress. Your self-esteem and confidence will grow every time you take a step towards conquering a stressful life situation and you will have an increased sense of pride in yourself and your achievements. And you have to admit that there are few things in life more rewarding than learning and growing as a person, so get stuck in!

How to use this book

If you are stressed, you will probably not feel like doing a great deal of reading in order to find out how to reduce your stress levels. For this reason, this book has different categories in each section, depending on how much time you have.

If you are EXTREMELY STRESSED and have VERY LITTLE TIME to read:

Skip briefly through Part One and just do the questionnaire on page 27 to find out whether you are a stress-prone personality.

It would also be useful to check what your overall stress quotient is by filling in the questionnaire on page 37. Find out in which area you are most vulnerable – mental, emotional or physical. Then:

- Go to the quick fix section of the area where you had the highest number of points and start using at least two or three of the solutions.

- Next, check through the self-sabotage section to make sure you aren't inadvertently adding to your stress through negative attitudes or behaviour.

■ Have a health check with a nutritionist or kinesiologist to see if you can support your body by taking particular vitamins, minerals or herbs (*see page 140*), or send in a hair sample to have it checked (*see Useful Addresses, page 168*).

■ If you are in the danger zone of having a breakdown, go to the Useful Addresses section and find a therapist who can help you get over the worst. While you are getting outside help, read the rest of the book, including the food for thought sections.

If you are VERY STRESSED but are willing and able to invest SOME TIME into dealing with your stress:

Skip briefly through Part One and do the questionnaires on page 27 and page 37. Note in which area you are most vulnerable – mental, emotional or physical.

■ Start with the practical exercises section of the area with your highest score on the stress quotient test. If, for example, your score was highest in the emotional area, start working with the exercises on pages 70–76 as a priority, but also start using the exercises in the other sections (mental, physical). At the same time, also check whether you are making life difficult for yourself without knowing it by reading the self-sabotage sections.

■ Scan through the quick fix and food for thought sections and see if you need to implement any of them to reduce your stress levels.

■ Make sure you know whether you are deficient in any vitamins or minerals. Check with a nutritionist or have a hair sample analysed (*see Useful Addresses, page 168*).

■ Read the food for thought sections when you have time.

■ Read Part One of the book in more detail when you can.

If you want to use this book as STRESS PREVENTION or if you are off work with a stress-related problem and have LOTS OF TIME:
Read the book from cover to cover.

Another way of using the book, of course, is to just see what catches your eye on the contents page. We are usually attracted by something that relates to what we need to know more about. Feel free to dip in and out of the book. Even though *Total Stress Relief* is a book about stress, it doesn't have to be a stressful experience to read!

PART ONE

Stress Signals

CHAPTER ONE

Recognising stress

A bit of excitement in life is fun – we all like it. Tackling something new or getting to grips with a challenging situation can be a rewarding experience, make you stronger and more confident and add to your life skills. As long as there is a balance between challenges and rest periods in your life, you are fine. A bit of pressure is useful and even necessary to keep your mental and physical coping mechanisms oiled and working. Use it or lose it!

It is only when pressure starts mounting to the extent where you cannot relax any more that we speak of 'stress'. Bear in mind, though, that this transition point from beneficial pressure to detrimental stress is not the same for everyone! Stress perception can vary enormously from one person to the next, depending on a number of factors, the most important of which is your *attitude*. You may assume that having a pile of paperwork on your desk or lots of deadlines is very stressful, but that is not necessarily the case. If you are highly motivated and very involved in what you are doing, you may actually feel positively elated by your work, even though there might be an awful lot to do. When you feel motivated to do a job, it is much less likely that you will feel stressed by the pressure. It is only when pressure *distresses* us that it turns into stress. If you have pressures in your life but can remain calm, you will stay healthy and cope better with the demands life makes on you.

Clearly, we cannot always choose what pressures life will

throw our way. You may have been made redundant or encounter unexpected financial difficulties; your children might start giving you problems or you and your new boss don't see eye to eye. As you can't draw a winning lottery ticket or a new job out of your hat, you will have to find ways of coping that allow you to stay intact physically and mentally. How to do this will be explained in Part Two of this book.

Generally speaking, stress is caused by an abnormal demand on our ability to adapt. Psychologists have attempted to draw up a list that grades the amount of readjustment that is needed in a number of life situations to indicate how much stress we might be under when this life event occurs. The scale most widely used is Holmes and Rahe's Social Readjustment Rating Scale. The scale measures Life Change Units (LCUs), with the death of a spouse given the arbitrary value of 100 LCUs. Other sources of stress are measured in relation to this.

Holmes and Rahe's Social Readjustment Rating Scale

Family

Death of spouse	100
Divorce	73
Marital separation	65
Death of close family member	63
Marriage	50
Marital reconciliation	45
Major change in health of family member	44
Pregnancy	40
Gaining new family member	39
Major change in number of arguments with spouse	35
Child leaving home	29
Troubles with in-laws	29
Spouse starting or ending work	26
Major change in number of family get-togethers	15

Personal

Jail sentence	63
Major injury or illness	53

Sexual difficulties	39
Death of close friend	37
Outstanding personal achievement	28
Major change in living conditions	25
Major revision of personal habits	24
Moving house	20
Major change in recreation	19
Major change in social activities	18
Major change in sleeping habits	16
Major change in eating habits	15
Holiday	13
Christmas	12
Minor violation of the law (e.g. traffic offence)	11

Work

Being fired	47
Retirement	45
Major business adjustment	39
Changing to new line of work	36
Major change in responsibilities	29
Trouble with boss	23
Major change in working conditions	20

Financial

Major change in financial state	38
Large mortgage or loan	31
Mortgage foreclosure	30
Small mortgage or loan	17

If you have a look through the above list and count how many LCU points you have gathered throughout 12 months, it will give you an idea of how much change you have to deal with. It is claimed that a score of more than 150 LCU points in any one year is associated with at least a 50/50 chance of a major health breakdown in the following year.

We all have a need to maintain physical and emotional equilibrium. When we are on an even keel, we feel comfortable and happy. When changes occur, our equilibrium is threatened and the body automatically strives to 'iron out' the imbalance. Let me explain this with an example. Say you have been working quite happily in an office where your responsibilities are clearly laid out and you have adequate time to meet your deadlines and finish your projects. You feel in control, you feel confident and strong. Now the company cuts back on their workforce. You are relieved to hear that you have kept your job, but now you will have to do two people's work because your colleague has been made redundant. All of a sudden, there is double the amount of work for you to do, but the deadlines still stay the same. The mere *thought* of having to achieve this Herculean task makes you feel stressed. At this point, the stress response has entered Phase One: your mind switches into *alarm mode*, and this makes your body switch into overdrive. Consequently, the muscles tense, adrenalin pumps through the system and blood pressure rises. All these heightened mental and physical responses help create increased energy so that the challenge can be met, but this state of overdrive cannot go on indefinitely.

The fight-or-flight response of the alarm stage is usually only short term. In order to allow the body to continue fighting, your system now enters Phase Two, which is called the 'resistance reaction'. Cortico-steroids are secreted by the adrenals to help maintain the energy supply by converting protein to energy and by retaining sodium, which helps maintain blood pressure. Depending on how stress-resilient you are, your body can cope for a while, but the time comes where your ability to adapt to the heightened demands on you gives way. You now enter Phase Three: *exhaustion*. As you can imagine, if your capacity to adapt to pressure is in overdrive for too long, it can make you ill. Once the hormones released from the adrenal glands become depleted due to overusage, the organs in the body start to weaken. If you look after elderly relatives all by yourself without getting any support, you can easily become unwell yourself. If you are in a relationship where you are continuously criticised or put down, it will eventually wear you down. In extreme cases, prolonged exposure to pressure that distresses you can lead to a mental or physical breakdown.

This means that you need to pay attention to your *distress* levels in any given situation. Once you feel distressed, you will be stressed. It doesn't matter what anyone else tells you about that situation ('But he does mean well, dear!') – when you are getting upset about what is going on around you, you need to take action. This means that either you have to change the situation or you have to change your attitude towards the situation. It is no good thinking that you should not be stressed. You are or you aren't, so be honest about it. Work through the stress-busting exercises in Part Two whenever you can, and you will start seeing positive results very soon.

SOS signals

Stress may affect you on a physical, mental or emotional level. The area that is your weakest link is where you will notice the overload effects first, depending on your personal disposition. Scan through the lists of physical, mental, emotional and behavioural warning signs that follow (*see pages 16–24*) and you will be able to establish quite easily in which area you are most vulnerable to stress.

How stress is activated

When unforeseen events or overload situations arise that put a strain on your ability to cope, you can start feeling out of control. It is this feeling of not being in charge of a particular situation that creates what we perceive as stress.

It now becomes very important to know how to deal with this stress so that you can handle the situation constructively and feel back in control. If you end up feeling that you were unable to successfully deal with the situation, you will begin to become nervous about the same or similar situations arising again in the future. In this respect, it does not matter what the situation was – it may have been something as simple as a casual remark that hurt you, but as long as it made you feel physically or emotionally out of control, a vicious circle will have been set up. Once you start to get afraid of the same situation occurring again, you tense up, you think about what happened and go over it again and again in your mind. The stress has now extended into the non-stress areas of your life, simply because you can't stop thinking about it, even though the situation has passed. By way of self-protection, you now begin to fear or avoid similar situations. And when you find yourself in a similar place, when you experience similar body sensations or when a similar event occurs, you will feel stressed. This can sometimes happen even if you have not thought about the original stressful event for a long time. The moment your subconscious mind perceives an upcoming event as potentially threatening, it switches you into stress-mode.

Successful stress management: fear of flying

Simone (32) came to see me for hypnotherapy for a great fear of flying. She had been flying a lot in the past, both for business and for pleasure. A year ago, she had started developing a phobia, but she had no idea why that was. The flight had been smooth and nothing exceptional had happened while she was up in the air. She was concerned that her fear was severely hampering her career prospects. Although she had been able to get away with taking trains or sending a colleague in her place, she knew she could not go on like this.

When we looked at the original occurrence under hypnosis, Simone remembered how she had been very agitated on that business trip because she had just had a big row with her partner and was afraid the relationship might break up as a consequence. On the flight back, she felt even more anxious, wondering whether her partner would still be there when she got home. Even though the relationship didn't break up until much later that year, Simone was 'stuck' with the feeling of anxiety when flying. Her subconscious mind had made the connection 'flying = anxiety' and faithfully produced these feelings every time she needed to fly.

Simone's case was quite straightforward after we found this subconscious connection. It took just two sessions for her to be able to go back to flying without worrying about it.

When you look at what is stressing you, what are the thought processes behind your stress? Is your stress pattern today a repeat of something that happened in the past? Where and when did you learn to believe that stress is the only way to react to the situation you are in today?

In Part Two, we will be looking at how you can resolve stress patterns that go back to past events.

The physical stress component

Different people react differently to stress, but the physiological responses are the same for everyone once they reach their individual stress threshold. As soon as we perceive a situation as potentially threatening, our primitive fight-or-flight response springs into action. The sympathetic nervous system kicks in and the breathing rate increases, providing the muscles with more oxygen, the heart rate increases, blood pressure rises, sugars and fats are released into the bloodstream for extra energy, the digestive processes close down and perspiration increases. Adrenalin and cortisol are released to mobilise the body, and all our senses are on red alert.

These automatic physical responses are great when you are trying to escape a house fire. They are less helpful when you are merely *thinking* about a presentation you have to give tomorrow. When you are in danger and have to run, all the extra adrenalin in the body is put to good use. If you are getting all uptight about your presentation, all the excess energy has nowhere to go. As you sit there worrying about your speech, your stress hormones go round and round in your system, keeping everything buzzing in overdrive. This makes it less likely that you will perform well the next day, simply because your body and mind are already out of balance even though nothing has happened yet!

The odd surge of adrenalin won't do you any harm, but if your stress response kicks in on a regular or even daily basis, your body's ability to adapt becomes overstretched. Normally, once the stress is over, the parasympathetic nervous system will reverse the physical stress responses by slowing down the heart rate, restimulating digestion, closing the pores and helping the bronchi contract again. When you are in overdrive all the time, the parasympaticus never gets the opportunity to rebalance the body's energies, and this increases the risk of exhaustion and heart and kidney problems, besides compromising your immune system.

To help you recognise stress symptoms more easily, read through the following list. Do any of these physical symptoms ring a bell?

tension in jaws, shoulders, stomach, chest

headaches

palpitations

breathlessness when resting

fidgeting

tics

dry mouth

sweating

dizziness

exhaustion

stomach ache and 'butterflies' in stomach

nausea

increased need to urinate

diarrhoea

sleeping problems

sexual problems

increased sensitivity to noise

sensitivity to bright lights

frequent infections

fluctuations in blood sugar levels

Successful stress management: nausea

Richard (25) had just started his new job when he was asked to attend a meeting with senior management. He was introduced to everyone by his boss and the meeting started. Having worked for a small company before, Richard felt a little uncomfortable sitting in a round with a great number of high-powered executives. As he was new to his position, he was unable to contribute to the discussion. He didn't have a problem with this fact, but the mere thought of having to contribute in future meetings made him feel very uneasy.

When the next meeting was scheduled, Richard noticed that he started feeling physically unwell, almost as if he was going to be sick. He was also aware of a sense of nervousness, although he couldn't say why. As his nausea before meetings persisted, he decided to seek help.

In his session with me, Richard learned first of all to relax by using self-hypnosis. This alone resulted in him feeling considerably calmer both before and during meetings. In addition, I taught him the Crown Pull and the Overload Soother to help him clear his head, both of which he used on a few more occasions before meetings. After two months, he had found his feet and regained his confidence sufficiently to be able to attend meetings without suffering from nausea.

More about the methods Richard used can be found on page 48 (self-hypnosis), page 47 (Crown Pull) and page 70 (Overload Soother).

The mental stress component

But it is not only the body that suffers when we are stressed. Body and mind always work in tandem. Whatever concerns one will automatically also influence the other. When your body goes into overdrive, so does your mind.

The first signs of mental stress are usually racing thoughts and problems concentrating. As a knock-on effect, it becomes harder to remember old and new information. You literally feel 'muddle-headed', you make more mistakes and this in turn creates even more stress! Your judgement is impaired and you are more likely to make rash decisions just to get a problem out of the way. Responsibilities that were once perfectly acceptable now become a chore and a burden.

Curiously, mental overdrive can be quite addictive. Even though it makes you lose perspective to constantly race ahead of yourself in your mind, some people thrive on it. This, of course, is not necessarily stress. Remember that we defined stress as being 'pressure coupled with distress'. If you are enjoying the buzz of having your mind race ahead of you, then that is fine. You only need to do something about it if it makes you feel ill, unhappy or out of control.

Even if you do enjoy mental overdrive, you may find it hard to stop thinking and worrying excessively. This could be simply because you don't know how to stop your thought processes from running away with you.

Here are some signs that will alert you to the fact that you are mentally stressed:

lack of concentration

forgetfulness

inability to remember recent events

inability to take in new information

inability to remember what you have just done

lack of co-ordination

mind going around in circles

indecisiveness

irrational or rash decision-making

being disorganised when normally you are well-organised

making more mistakes than usual

becoming very fussy

struggling with simple tasks

Successful stress management: poor memory

Liz (48) had been working for 20 years in her job as shop assistant for a big chain of retailers. She had always enjoyed her work and was very concerned when her company experienced a severe downturn in sales which resulted in a large number of people being made redundant. Although Liz considered herself lucky that she had been kept on, she began to feel quite stressed by the fact that her workload had doubled within a very short period of time. Regular working hours became a thing of the past and Liz felt she was losing control over the amount of work that faced her every day.

After two months of daily overtime, Liz noticed that she was making lots of mistakes because she found it increasingly difficult to concentrate. She felt unable to take in and retain information she was given by her supervisor so that important tasks were not carried out correctly. One day, Liz even forgot to put an address on an envelope that was to go out to another branch. She had already had a warning and was becoming very worried about losing her job if her memory kept letting her down.

In her sessions with me, Liz learnt how to relax her body and calm her mind by using the Overload Soother and the Pyramid of Peace. A breathing exercise and the Crown Pull helped her brain to become adequately supplied with cerebro-spinal fluid and oxygen once again, and soon Liz's memory had improved significantly.

More about the methods Liz used can be found on page 74 (Pyramid of Peace), page 70 (Overload Soother), page 70 (Under-8-Breathing) and page 47 (Crown Pull).

The emotional stress component

When body and mind are having a hard time coping with difficult circumstances, the emotions will soon follow suit. Body, mind and emotions are very closely interlinked. A physical illness (body) can make you depressed (emotion), an allergy (body) can make you feel anxious (emotions), and emotional upset can affect your work performance (mind) and your health (body).

The emotional side-effects of stress can encompass anything from aggression to depression. When pressure builds up too much, some people can virtually change personality. Where they were once patient and tolerant, now they are on a short fuse and give others a hard time over everything. Where they were once positive and optimistic, now they are cynical and become dejected over even minor hitches.

Stress can bring out the worst in people and emotional changes are usually negative. Your personality type and general disposition will dictate how these emotional changes progress. Some people become depressed and lose confidence, others feel anxious or even panicky and struggle with feelings of guilt about their perceived inadequacy, still others become morose and withdrawn from friends and family. A perspective distorted by stress often results in an altered perception of yourself and others. As you begin to feel dejected and incompetent, you start disliking yourself and you begin to suspect that others feel the same about you. Some people find it difficult to express their feelings about how stress is getting to them. Instead, they shout, cry or drive like a maniac. This usually results in a vicious circle where their fear of being disliked becomes reality as a result of their behaviour. This in turn creates even more stress: 'I *knew* nobody liked me and here's the proof!'

Emotional problems can of course also be a result of something that has happened to you many years ago. Past trauma can have a lasting effect on your ability to function fully on the mental and emotional level. The past can stress you for the rest of your life unless you tackle the old issues that still rule your life today. This is usually best done with the help of a qualified therapist, but there are also a number of things you can do to help yourself. More about this in Part Two of the book.

Here are some signs that show you that stress is affecting your emotions:

anxiety

depression

phobias

panic and panic attacks

aggression

feeling persecuted

cynicism

negativity

fearing the worst

guilt

mood swings

weepiness

nightmares

feeling abandoned

excessive worrying

loss of sense of humour

Successful stress management: fear

Susan (38) was a mother of two who had given up her job as a secretary to fully dedicate herself to her children. With both children at school now, she decided to return to work part-time but felt that the 10-year gap since she last worked had dented her confidence. Would she be able to deal with all the new technology that had come in while she had been away? Her last job had been with a very small firm which had an old-fashioned computer but no internet.

Susan worried so much about her potential inadequacies that she could not even bring herself to look at newspaper ads or follow up some promising leads for part-time jobs that came her way.

In her sessions, we worked on reducing her anxiety levels generally as Susan, according to her own assessment, was a fairly nervous person anyway. She learnt to relax and to tap away her negative emotions with the Stress Tap and to help her breathing come down to a relaxed level. Within three weeks, she was actively looking for a job, and after six weeks, she had started work again. *More about the methods Susan used can be found on page 74 (Pyramid of Peace), page 72 (Stress Tap) and page 70 (Under-8-Breathing).*

The behavioural stress component

When pressure becomes too great and you feel out of control and struggle to keep going, your behaviour may also be affected. Rather than becoming emotional as a result to an overload, some people start displaying uncharacteristic or exaggerated reactions and behaviour. Most of us would readily recognise excessive smoking as stress-related behaviour, but did you know that stress can also be at the bottom of obsessive behaviour or compulsive thoughts?

Our behaviour and reactions are governed by three factors – personality, past experiences and present circumstances. Your personality will determine what behavioural *tendencies* you are likely to display when under pressure. If you have an addictive personality, you are more likely to start eating sweets or other food in larger quantities, drinking more heavily or smoking excessively. If you are an introvert who represses emotions and finds it hard to speak up, you might end up withdrawing even more when you are stressed.

Our past experiences will also have a bearing on how well we cope and whether we change our behaviour for the worse when we are pressurised. Whatever we have seen, heard or experienced in the past will have contributed to our attitudes, our beliefs and our self-perception.

Our present circumstances can also add to pressures that lead to changed behaviour. Even if you are stoic by nature, losing a loved one or experiencing grave financial difficulties will influence how you feel and behave. It will then be particularly important to cultivate a positive and constructive attitude in order to keep negative behavioural changes to a minimum.

Quite a few behavioural reactions to stress are an exaggerated version of something you are already in the habit of doing. If you have a tendency to overeat or bite your nails, you will find that in times of stress you start bingeing and reducing your nails to half their size.

Here are some of the behavioural signs that tell you that your stress levels have gone off the scale:

excessive smoking

excessive alcohol intake

overeating and bingeing

eating nothing at all

neglecting personal appearance

driving and/or speaking aggressively

withdrawing into yourself

avoiding social contact

starting lots of things without finishing anything

nailbiting

hair-pulling

skin picking

obsessive thoughts

compulsive actions (checking and rechecking locks, lights, taps etc.)

Successful stress management: obsessive thoughts

Catherine (20) attended one of my workshops because she wanted to deal with her obsession of having to check her gas cooker again and again to make sure she had really turned off the gas. She knew that her concern about the gas went far beyond common-sense caution, and yet she couldn't stop herself. Catherine admitted that she could not leave the flat without checking at least 10 times whether all the knobs on the cooker had been turned off properly. She felt that something awful would happen if she didn't check.

I asked Catherine to explain a little bit about her background. It turned out that her parents had not wanted her to move in with her boyfriend and were still giving her a hard time about it. As it happened, the parents were right – the boyfriend had turned out to be quite nasty and Catherine now found herself in a position where she did not want to admit that her parents had been right and wanted to try and make things work with the boyfriend, and this inner pressure seemed to have produced her obsession.

I asked Catherine to go out and buy herself a little exercise book. Every time she checked the cooker, she had to enter all the details in her book: time of day, *which* knob she had checked and whether she had turned it off properly. I also pointed out to her that advice is not necessarily wrong because it comes from your parents.

Two weeks after the workshop, Catherine wrote to me that she had stopped checking the cooker. 'I just couldn't be bothered with writing it all down all the time, so I decided it was easier to just stop checking,' she wrote. A little while later, she left her abusive boyfriend.

Stress resilience

Everyone reacts in their own way when things go wrong in life. Some people panic, others withdraw, others start blaming whoever they feel has caused their present problems. And some people simply get on and deal with the problem without too much emotional upheaval. Just look at drivers in a traffic jam: some drum the steering wheel in an irritated manner, others are chatting and laughing with their passengers, others just turn up their radio. Everyone is sitting in the same boat, but not everyone is cut out to be the ideal companion if it were a lifeboat!

So what is it that makes some people so stress-resilient? Over the years I found that there are four qualities that are indispensable if you want to cope well with great pressure. These inner strengths are:

- keeping your emotions in check

- staying physically as relaxed as possible

- taking constructive action

- using common sense

Later on, you will find a questionnaire that helps you decide how stress-resilient you are, but before we move on to that, I'd like to explain in a little more detail about those four qualities.

Keeping your emotions in check

This may appear to be a tall order when you feel that you have just had the shock of your life. Your wife has just gone off with someone else, your boss piles another load of work on your desk when you can hardly cope with what you have already, you get a tax demand which is three times higher than expected – it is perfectly natural to feel confused, upset or numb with shock. However, it is *essential* to come out of that emotion, whatever it is, because while you stay distressed, you cannot deal with the situation constructively.

In Chapter 4 you will find ways of dealing with your emotions that allow you to recover from stress quickly and easily.

Staying physically as relaxed as possible

As emotions have a direct impact on the body and all its processes, you will also have to look after the physical side. You will notice that once you have toned down your emotions, your body will follow by relaxing and harmonising itself. However, sometimes it can be a good idea to actively help the body rebalance itself while at the same time working on the emotions. That way you tackle the stress problems from two angles.

If you think you cannot afford the time to do any relaxation exercises, let me tell you that you cannot afford *not* to do them! But as I'm only too well aware that it is hard to carve out time in a day that is already crammed full of tasks and obligations, I have made sure that the relaxation exercises in this book are relatively short while still being effective.

Taking constructive action

Stress-resilient people are doers. They are able to assess calmly what the problem is and look at the options they have. Once they have selected an option, they start implementing it as quickly as possible. This does not mean that stress-resilient people are all cold fish who suppress their emotions. Like everyone else, they feel pressure, a sense of alarm or even pain. The big difference is that they don't confuse pain with suffering. Pain in life is unavoidable, suffering is optional. There is no virtue in suffering; it just delays you moving on with your life. It is by avoiding positive action that pain turns into suffering. If you are unhappy with your partner or feel you are being treated unfairly at work, you need to do something about it. You need to speak about what is bothering you, renegotiate a better deal for yourself or leave the situation that is making you unhappy. Not taking action will only prolong the agony.

Using common sense

This can be difficult in a crisis or when you feel very emotional about an event. We all have seen a friend fall in love with someone who is clearly unsuitable for them and yet they are adamant that this is the right person. A friend of mine was stood up, put down and ignored by a man who wouldn't come and see her when she was ill, even though he was passing through her part of town. And yet she insisted that he was the right man for her. When it finally became too much even for her, she managed to step back and see how selfish he was. At this point, she was finally able to let go of him.

When we are in the middle of an unhappy life situation, it can be difficult to see the wood for the trees. So it becomes crucial to step back and get a more detached view of what is happening in your life.

Are you a stress-prone personality?

So, how well are you doing when it comes to tackling stress? Do you have the necessary stamina to withstand emotional upheaval? How about when it comes to putting your thoughts and words into action? Find out how vulnerable you are to stress by answering the following questions.

Stress-prone personality questionnaire

This questionnaire should be filled in with great care. Please take your time over every single question and really think about your answer. The questionnaire is designed to show up what tendencies you have rather than how you are all the time, so bear that in mind when you decide whether to tick the 'yes' or the 'no' box.

Yes No

Do you find it difficult to hide your feelings when you are annoyed or distressed about something? ☐ ☐

Yes No

Looking at the second hand of your watch, do you take more than eight breaths a minute when you are resting? ☐ ☐

Do you often feel dizzy or breathless even though you have not exerted yourself? ☐ ☐

Do you tend to finish other people's sentences for them? ☐ ☐

Do you often interrupt others while they are speaking? ☐ ☐

Do you react physically to stressful events? ☐ ☐

When you hear unwelcome news, do you feel as though someone had punched you in the stomach? ☐ ☐

Do you feel very strongly for others? ☐ ☐

Does it generally take you a long time to take positive action about a stressful situation? ☐ ☐

Would you do anything for a quiet life? ☐ ☐

Do hesitant or insecure people drive you nuts? ☐ ☐

Do you prefer it when other people take the lead when it comes to making decisions? ☐ ☐

Do you easily get confused or frightened? ☐ ☐

Do you frequently have arguments with other people? ☐ ☐

Do you find it nearly impossible to say 'no'? ☐ ☐

Do other people seem to ignore it when you say 'no'? ☐ ☐

Does it frighten you when others disagree with you? ☐ ☐

	Yes	No
Do you frequently suffer from a racing heart, even though there is nothing wrong with your heart?	☐	☐
Do even ordinary chores make you feel tired?	☐	☐
Are you very concerned what others think of you?	☐	☐
Do you fidget or bite your nails?	☐	☐
Do you experience frequent headaches or persistent pains in your back and neck?	☐	☐
Do you have problems sleeping?	☐	☐
Have you lost interest in sex?	☐	☐
Do you often feel indecisive?	☐	☐
Do you feel like a failure?	☐	☐
Are you worried that something dreadful might happen in your life?	☐	☐
Have you lost your sense of humour?	☐	☐
Do you have problems concentrating and remembering?	☐	☐
Are your personal standards very high and demanding?	☐	☐
Does it throw you when your daily routine is disrupted?	☐	☐
Do you feel awkward when with new people?	☐	☐
Do you find it difficult to leave a situation when you have had enough?	☐	☐
Do you usually put yourself last?	☐	☐
Do imperfections upset you?	☐	☐
Do you often not finish what you started?	☐	☐

	Yes	No
Do you find it difficult to switch off at the end of your day?	☐	☐
Do you neglect your relationships over your work commitments?	☐	☐
Do you neglect your own needs because you are wrapped up in your work or looking after someone else?	☐	☐
Does the amount of work you have to do every day seem to overpower you?	☐	☐
Do you feel undervalued by your boss, your family or your partner?	☐	☐

Please add up how many times you ticked 'yes':

0–3
You are a personality type who is quite robust when it comes to stress. You are not easily thrown and are likely to handle difficult situations in a constructive manner. You might as well give this book to someone who really needs it!

4–10
You are not doing too badly, especially if you are at the lower end of the scale. If you are nearer the 10-point mark, you need to start watching out a little. You have a certain streak of vulnerability in your emotional make-up, maybe as a result of what has happened previously in your life. This vulnerability could lay you open to unwelcome stress reactions when the going gets tough. Work with the exercises in Part Two to make yourself more stress-resilient.

11–20
Alarm bells are ringing! Your emotional make-up makes you susceptible to stress responses on all levels – mental, emotional and physical. Are there events in the past that have

knocked your confidence? What is it that has made you feel you are not good enough? Working through the exercises in Part Two is a *must*. Please don't delay getting to work. The quality of your life can improve dramatically if you are prepared to put some work into it.

Over 20

You have lived through a lot of things in your life that have severely affected your self-esteem and confidence. In all likelihood there is some unfinished business in your past. In addition to doing the exercises in this book, you may want to consider seeking professional help from a good therapist or counsellor. (*See Useful Addresses, page 166.*)

PART TWO

Stress Busting

CHAPTER TWO

Assessing your stress levels

Life is 10 per cent what happens to you and 90 per cent how you react to it. The way you react reflects your attitude, and your attitude is based on what you believe to be true. This does not mean that what you believe *is* actually true, just that you *believe* it to be true. It may be totally untrue. I had a client a few years ago who was convinced she was ugly even though she had a well-paid job as a model. Another client felt that it would jeopardise his standing at work if he asked for assistance with his workload. When he finally did ask, not only was he given help, but he was also offered a promotion half a year later.

Your attitude is vital if you want to get through stressful times in one piece. So, if you think your beliefs are holding you back, question them. Are they really true? What makes you think they are true? How would your life be if your negative beliefs were not true? Any belief that starts with 'I can't' or 'I couldn't possibly' is inaccurate. Replace those by 'I can learn how to …' Your beliefs may date all the way back to your childhood but that doesn't make them immutable. You cannot change what happened to you in the past, but you can certainly change the way you feel about it. In other words, you can change your attitude towards what has happened in the past, and this will allow you to move forward and away from old ways.

Beliefs are like a prison, but they are a prison without walls. This prison only has lines on the floor which mark the ground around you. Inside the lines are your old ideas. Outside are new ideas that invite you to step over and escape your prison. Dare to try the new ideas! You have nothing to lose but your stress!

Doing things differently from the way you have done them before is *not* difficult. The only reason you experience stress is because you *expect* things to be difficult. In order to change your attitude, you only have to change your mind. *Decide* that from now on certain situations are a doddle, and they will be. Think of something that you really like doing – maybe a hobby you have or a particular computer game you like to play. Chances are that you knew little about it when you started off. But because you were interested, you started reading up on the subject and trying out things, and you would not have dreamed of perceiving this as stressful – on the contrary! If we are interested in something, we can keep going for hours and often resent having to go to bed and sleep because this interrupts our spending time with our new interest. It is a bit like being in love and begrudging anything that interrupts daydreaming about the other person. Once you have *decided* to lighten up about your stressful situation, life becomes a lot easier.

In this chapter, you will find a way of assessing your current stress levels by finding your stress quotient (SQ). Knowing your SQ will allow you to check your progress as you tackle your stress issues.

The following chapters offer you mental, emotional and physical solutions. All these areas are of course very closely interlinked and cannot therefore be entirely separated from one another. An emotional stress reaction will always have a physical component, just as a mental stress reaction can also affect the emotions.

If you are pressed for time, I suggest you work out your present SQ and then delve straight into the quick fixes or practical exercises that relate to your particular stress problems. If you have more time, include the food for thought and self-sabotage sections in your reading. This will help you look in greater depth at why you may have developed certain attitudes and beliefs that hold you back or make you more stress-prone.

What is your stress quotient?

Before trying to remedy a problem, it is a good idea to establish where you stand at the moment. Establishing the status quo gives you an opportunity to assess how serious your problem is. At times, it will help you see that your problem is not as serious as you thought it was! When you are caught up in a difficult situation, you can lose your perspective, so it can be helpful to have a reference point against which to match your current experience.

Stress quotient questionnaire

In order to help you assess your stress levels, I have devised a 10-point stress scale. To start with, please read carefully through each section.

Level 0: meditative state
Body	still, floating feeling
Mind	calm and focused or inactive
Emotions	calm, serene
Behaviour	inactive, passive

Level 0 can only be reached by resting, sleeping or meditating. This is when you are in perfect harmony with yourself and the world around you.

Level 1: serene state
Body	calm and comfortable
Mind	calm and focused, thinking clearly
Emotions	calm and serene, on an even keel
Behaviour	calm, relaxed movements, unhurried, unflappable

Level 1 is a great place to be! You are on top of things and feel in control of your life.

Level 2: happy state

Body	calm and relaxed
Mind	thinking clearly
Emotions	feeling on an even keel, happy
Behaviour	movements slow and deliberate

At level 2, you are comfortable and relaxed and function optimally.

Level 3: comfortable state

Body	calm and relaxed
Mind	thinking clearly
Emotions	happy
Behaviour	movements unhurried and co-ordinated

Level 3 is a good everyday state. If your body, mind, emotions and behaviour are even only 30 per cent of your waking hours on level 3, you are doing fine.

Level 4: busy state

Body	comfortably busy feeling
Mind	busy thinking, comfortable and fully in control
Emotion	occasional ups and downs
Behaviour	movements faster but co-ordinated

Level 4 is still a good state to be in and quite comfortable. It is a perfectly acceptable state as long as you make sure you get some relaxation during the day.

Level 5: light stress

Body	blood pressure goes up, feeling physically a bit tense
Mind	mild lack of concentration occasionally
Emotions	feeling slightly tense but still fully in control
Behaviour	regular ups and downs, movements fast and occasionally hurried, habits such as nailbiting and smoking become worse

It is at level 5 where stress starts. There is nothing to worry about yet, but please watch your habits now. Make sure you get enough sleep at night and take breaks during the day and you will be fine.

Level 6: stress build-up

Body   blood pressure is up, heart beating faster, but rest brings relief

Mind   occasional memory lapses

Emotions feeling hassled at times, impatient

Behaviour movements hurried, occasionally clumsy; habits such as smoking get out of hand occasionally

Level 6 is where you have to watch out. Things are starting to get out of control and you need to take action to control your stress levels. Make a concerted effort to keep time free for yourself and relax regularly.

Level 7: serious stress

Body   problems sleeping, difficulties switching off

Mind   memory severely impaired, frequent problems concentrating

Emotions frequently upset and agitated

Behaviour movements hurried, uncoordinated, often dropping items or bumping into things, habits are out of control

At level 7, stress has started to get the upper hand. Take time out and think how you can reorganise your life or make some changes. Warning bells are beginning to ring. Please don't just turn them off – they are there for a reason.

Level 8: danger signals

Body   insomnia for more than three days in a row, very tired during the day, rest brings very little refreshment

Mind   unable to think clearly

Emotions losing your cool easily, feeling depressed

Behaviour frequently aggressive, gritting teeth, snapping at people or being excessively self-critical

Level 8 tells you that you cannot go on like this without doing damage to either your body or mind. Your stress levels are out of control and so are your feelings. You are no longer effective in what you are doing.

Level 9: exhaustion

Body   constant insomnia, exhausted during the day, agitated when trying to rest

Mind   constant negative and critical thoughts

Emotions   waking up exasperated, dreading the day, losing your cool all the time and in inappropriate situations

Behaviour   erratic, unpredictable, no longer yourself

At level 9, you are only one step away from a nervous breakdown. Seek professional help *now*!

Level 10: breakdown

Body   unable to get out of bed, too weak to do simple things like making a cup of tea

Mind   blank, switched off

Emotions   totally blank, feeling like a vegetable

Behaviour   frozen, unable to react to anything any more

Immediate medical attention is required. It takes years to fully recover from this state, so don't let things come to this!

Your stress score

Now go through all the sections again and jot down your stress level for each of the categories: physical, mental, emotional and behavioural. Don't expect to have all the scores in the same category – it is perfectly possible that you are physically at level 6, but emotionally at level 4 and mentally at level 3 for example.

My stress scores:

Body:
Mind:
Emotions:
Behaviour:

How did you do?

Now add up the points in all four categories and divide the result by four. This is your stress quotient.

Example:	Body	5
	Mind	7
	Emotions	5
	Behaviour	8

$$25 \div 4 = 6.25$$

This means your stress quotient (SQ) is around 6.

Your stress quotient

Your SQ gives you your overall stress levels. Here is what your SQ means.

SQ below 3.0

You are doing well. There is no immediate need to do any of the exercises in Part Two. However, life doesn't always run smoothly and you may find it useful to familiarise yourself with at least some of the physical exercises now so you know how to do them when you need them.

SQ 3.1–4.5

Still OK, but a slight tendency towards stress. Concentrate on those exercises that relate to your weakest areas. That way, you need to do very little to comfortably get your quotient down to 3.0 or below.

SQ 4.6–6

You are stressed, but things are still under control, as long as you don't ignore the early warning signals you are getting now. Aim to get your SQ down to 4.0 or slightly lower if you can. That way you have a little more breathing space if additional pressures build up.

SQ 6–7.5

You have been having warning signs for a while but have ignored them or didn't know what to do to reduce your stress levels. It's a good job you bought this book! Start working on your main stress areas now and initially make it your aim to get down to 6 or just below. Once you have reduced your SQ to that level, work on bringing it down further.

SQ 7.6–8.5

Your stress levels are out of control or very close to it. Make sure stress does not take over your life. Just popping a pill to mute the symptoms won't work in the long run. Make your stress control exercises your number one priority.

SQ over 8.6

Unless you take time off now and make some major changes to your life or to your attitude, you will become ill. If you can't do it on your own, seek professional help.

CHAPTER THREE

Strengthening mental resilience

Even though mind, emotions and body are all closely inter-linked and always work together, I would like to separate them out for you to help you distinguish more clearly between them. When I speak about the mind, I refer to your mental capacities, that is your ability to concentrate, to take in new information, to remember old and new information and to be in a position to think logically. You need your mental capacity in order to study, to work, to impose a constructive and work-able order on your life, and to make rational day-to-day decisions. For example, if you had the choice of walking to work or taking the car, the fact that it was raining hard and you had a cold could lead you to the decision that it was better to take the car. That would be a rational decision based on the prevailing circumstances.

The mind is the rational, logical part of you that helps you to make unemotional choices, to store and retrieve information and to order and calculate. It is the counterpart to the emotions. A good example of the interplay between mind and emotions is exam nerves. Your mental capacity has helped you retain what you have revised – you 'know your stuff'. If you now enter the exam room and start getting emotional by expecting difficulties and imagining failure, all of a sudden the carefully stored infor-mation is no longer available. Your emotions have barred the way to your inner information store.

For many people, lack of concentration and a bad memory are the first signs that their mind is affected by stress. Do you find yourself reacting in any of the following ways?

- You find it difficult to concentrate on things.

- Your memory is letting you down frequently.

- You have lots of different things on your mind but cannot grasp a clear thought.

- You are often undecided these days and this is untypical for you.

- You make irrational or rash decisions which, on reflection, don't make any sense to you later on.

- You take longer to do tasks that you were able to do quite quickly before.

- You start lots of things but don't finish any.

Clearly, the better you deal with stress, the less your mental capacity will be affected. The following exercises will help you build better stress resilience and rebalance yourself if your mental capacity has already started to suffer due to stress.

Mental quick fixes

- Put on some music you like and dance through the room. This creative activity exercises the right side of the brain and helps rebalance your brain.

- Get a fish tank and watch the fish swim around languidly. This allows your mind to calm down.

- Write down all your worries. Putting them on a piece of paper gets them out of your head.

- Get out into nature and walk.

- Concentrate on what is right now rather than what *might* happen tomorrow.

- Sing in the bath and use the shampoo bottle as a microphone.

- Nobody is perfect, and who wants to be nobody? Mistakes are OK.

- Delete the phrase 'I can't' from your vocabulary. It isn't constructive and blocks your view of possible solutions.

- Replace worries with hope and action.

- Write a few lines with your other hand. This rebalances the two hemispheres of the brain.

- Expect to be lucky.

Practical exercises

Short meditation 1

- Make yourself comfortable and close your eyes.

- Out of the following, choose a word that symbolises 'calmness' to you: 'harmony', 'tranquillity', 'serenity', 'peace', 'relax'.

- Meditate on your chosen word. Visualise scenes that tie in with the word or build up mental images that illustrate the word. You can also spend some time imagining what it would feel like if you experienced harmony or tranquillity inside yourself.

- Open your eyes again.

Short meditation 2

- Pick a material such as dress fabric, a stone, a piece of wood or anything else that appeals to you.

- With your eyes closed, explore the texture of this material.

- Spend at least two minutes doing this.

Stop overthinking

When tasks and pressures start building up, the mind can sometimes go into overdrive. Many of my clients say, 'I wish there was a switch in my head that I could flick and turn off all the thoughts going around in my mind!' For some, this switch consists of a tablet they take to calm them down, but that is not really a long-term solution. So let me introduce you to a simple mental technique to stop yourself from overthinking:

- Say to yourself repeatedly during the day: 'I have no expectations and I will deal with whatever happens *when* it happens.'

Yes, that's all there is to it. Let me explain why this works.

When you think about a stressful day that lies in front of you, your thoughts run approximately like this: 'Oh my God, I have so much to do! I must do X and Y and Z, and after that, A and B needs to get sorted out as well! I don't know how I'm going to do it all. I won't even have time to eat!' Basically, the day hasn't even started but you are already in a tizz. What is happening is that your mind is racing ahead of you and *anticipating* how tired and stressed you will feel once you have completed all the tasks ahead. These frantic thought processes first thing in the morning start sapping your energy, so that you are launching into a busy day with only half your normal energy at your disposal. Then, when you end up shattered at the end of the day, you seem to have proved that you were right all along – you had a dreadful day and you feel physically drained.

In order to have the maximum energy available at the start of a busy day, use 'I have no expectations and I will deal with whatever happens *when* it happens' as a form of mantra. You will notice how your body starts relaxing at the thought of 'no expectations'. This relaxation tells you that you have just stopped yourself from wasting valuable energy. You will feel calmer mentally and emotionally as a consequence.

Give your brain an oxygen hit

Half the problem with being stressed and unable to concentrate properly is that you don't breathe deeply enough to supply your brain with sufficient oxygen. When we get stressed, we tend to hold our breath or only breathe in a shallow way, using only the top part of our lungs. In order to deepen your breathing and get oxygen all the way up into the brain again, do the following exercise for two minutes:

- Rub both your hands together for a moment to create energy.

- Place your palms one on top of the other on the area just below your navel.

- Breathe consciously into your belly, making your palms rise with every in-breath.

- Imagine breathing oxygen into your brain.

The Crown Pull

When we breathe, there is a microscopic movement of the cranial bones which in turn allows the cerebro-spinal fluid to move freely through the spinal column and the skull. When we are tense or upset and don't breathe deeply enough, this can result in bones in the skull becoming slightly stuck together so that the fluid cannot circulate properly.

The Crown Pull influences the flow of cerebro-spinal fluid in a positive way. It helps calm your nervous system and can also often take away a headache or stress-induced stomach ache, as well as helping you think more clearly.

- Place both of your hands with your fingers like combs on top of your head so that your little fingers are touching your hairline at the front.

- Firmly press down onto your scalp and pull your fingers away from the midline, 'combing' outwards with each hand.

- Now place your hands in the same way higher up on the midline of the head and repeat the procedure.

- Now place hands even further back on your head, towards the crown, and repeat the procedure.

Self-hypnosis

If you have never been to a hypnotherapist you may feel mystified by the concept of hypnosis. And yet you enter a hypnotic state regularly, usually several times a day. Remember the last time you stared out of the window with a faraway look in your eyes, thinking about something very intently and switching off from your environment?

You can use this state to relieve mental stress. Try the following exercise. You can do it with your eyes open, but it is easier with your eyes closed.

- Settle back in a chair and close your eyes.

- Start counting backwards from 99 to 70. Count slowly to fit in with your breathing.

- Now count down from 69 to 30, while imagining walking down the steps of a beautiful staircase. *Feel* yourself walking down in time with your breathing. *See* the beautiful grand staircase stretching ahead of you. Imagine the steps are carpeted so that your progress is as effortless as possible.

- Count down from 29 to 0 while imagining drifting further down in a luxurious lift, as large as a room, carpeted, with views of landscapes outside. Watch the indicator panel of the lift, with the numbers decreasing steadily in time with your breathing.

- As you arrive at 0, the lift doors open and you enter a room that is furnished just as you would like it. It has all your favourite things in it and it is totally private. Find a comfortable chair in your room and settle back in it.

- Remain there in your imagination until you feel rested and refreshed, then open your eyes again.

The Screen Exercise

When emotions have taken you over, it can be near impossible to think clearly. Then it becomes very easy to make unwise decisions or to agree to something which is not to your advantage. The Screen Exercise shows you how to step back and emotionally detach yourself from your current situation so that you can see more clearly what is going on.

Taking an outsider's point of view and imagining another person in your situation will put a new perspective on your stress problem so you can evaluate more calmly what needs to be done.

- With your eyes closed, think about the situation that is currently causing you stress.

- Imagine projecting the situation onto a screen in your mind, as if it were a film you were watching. Include only what has really happened, *not* what you are afraid *might* happen!

- Replace yourself in the film with someone else of the same gender.

- Watch the film as an outside observer.
  How do you feel about what is going on in the film?
  What advice would you give the person who is
  replacing you on the screen?

- Open your eyes again and act on your own advice.

Anticipating success

When life gets a bit too hectic, we can end up feeling
mentally tied in knots. Nothing flows any more,
pessimism sets in and we cannot see a way out of our
current conundrum. As a consequence, we paint disaster
pictures about how it will all end, namely in tears. Not
the best way of getting more clear-headed and
composed!

The quickest way out of this mental state is to focus
your attention on something positive. And what better
mental image than the projection of a happy ending?

- Settle back in a chair and close your eyes.

- Imagine you can travel forward in time to the day
  when the current crisis is resolved.

- Experience with all your senses what it feels like to
  have resolved the problem and enjoy the resulting
  feelings of relief and elation.

- Hang on to the positive feelings and bring them back
  with you into the here and now.

- Open your eyes again.

Make sure you don't get all tangled up in considerations
about *how* the situation will resolve itself. The *how* will
look after itself as long as you keep your aim firmly in
mind. If you stay focused on a positive outcome, you can
think more clearly and you will make better decisions,
which will eventually lead to the desired results.

If there could be a number of different positive outcomes, then simply concentrate on visualising one version today and another version tomorrow. This is not an exercise in correctly predicting the future, but rather a way of clearing negative thoughts from your mind and focusing on a positive future.

Mental self-sabotage

Drugs and alcohol

Recreational drugs

One sure way of messing up your mind is by taking recreational drugs. I'm talking here about uppers, downers and hallucinogenic pills and weeds of any description as well as alcohol. Just because marijuana has been legalised in many countries does not mean that it does not interfere with your brain chemistry! Drugs may seem fun, they may calm you down or pep you up, they may take you away from the everyday world and give you amazing hallucinations, but they mess with your mind.

If you can only unwind by taking drugs, you need to think again. Apart from creating a dependency, you are also messing with your brain, particularly when you are popping pills or smoking weed. They are *not* harmless. They are chemicals that influence your brain. And your brain governs all your body processes, which in turn determine how clearly you can think and how adequately you can function. The latest research suggests that both recreational and medically prescribed mood-altering drugs such as antidepressants and 'happy' pills can lead to psychotic episodes which can take years to overcome. That is if you don't die first or do irreversible damage to your body.

Drugs are *not* the answer. They never have been and they never will be. If you like your brain the way it is, don't start on drugs or, if you have already started, stop as soon as you can. If you can't do it by yourself, get help. Stop playing Russian roulette with your brain!

To help yourself cut down and ultimately quit, have a think about the following:

- *When* do you use the substance? Is it a particular time of day? Why then?

- Is there a pattern to your use?

- *Why* do you need the substance? Is it to comfort yourself, to reward yourself or protect yourself from feeling certain feelings or needs?

- Can you get that comfort, reward or protection in a less harmful way?

- Keep a tab of your substance use and monitor your progress as you reduce it.

- Once you have started reducing your substance use, make sure you tackle problems straight away so they don't lead to a relapse.

- Don't let a relapse discourage you. Have another go!

- Get friends and family to support you by telling them that you are working on reducing drug use.

- If you can't cope, get outside help (*see Useful Addresses, page 166*).

Alcohol

When it comes to alcohol, there is certainly nothing wrong with moderate consumption, but for many people alcohol becomes a crutch when they feel stressed, and after a while it starts becoming a stressor itself. When you need your mind to be clear to deal with problems, alcohol is the worst thing you can put into your body. It is estimated that between 28,000 and 33,000 deaths a year in the UK are alcohol-related.

The question is: what constitutes moderate drinking? In men, this is considered to be anything up to 21 units per week; in women, 15 units over the same period of time. A standard unit is half a pint of standard beer, lager or cider (3–5%) or

25 ml of spirits (40%) or a 125 ml glass of wine (10–11%) or 60 ml of sherry or port (18–25%). Obviously, there are differences in the potency of drinks. A strong lager, even if it is only half a pint, would count as two standard drinks as opposed to an ordinary-strength lager, which would count as only one.

You are considered a heavy drinker if, as a man, you have more than 51 units per week and, as a woman, more than 36 units per week.

Women in particular seem to be drinking more today than ever before. Figures from the Office of National Statistics reveal that 21 per cent of women exceed the recommended limits of two to three units of alcohol per day on at least one day a week. Although women are still drinking a lot less than men, their alcohol intake is still increasing, whereas that of men has stabilised over the past 10 years.

The reason why, generally speaking, women can hold less drink than men is because of their higher fat-to-water ratio. This means that women are less able to dilute alcohol within the body and are therefore more prone to liver damage than men. Also, women are thought to have lower levels of alcohol dehyrogenase (ADH), an enzyme required in the metabolism of alcohol. The rule of thumb is that if you are well-built and muscular, you can tolerate more than if you are thin.

The detrimental effects of heavy alcohol consumption include:

alcohol dependency

high blood pressure

insomnia

obesity

higher risk of accidents

higher risk of strokes

high risk of foetal alcohol syndrome (baby has low IQ, facial abnormalities and central nervous system problems)

depression

liver disease and failure

increased risk of cancer (mouth and oesophagus)

pneumonia

Check against the following list to see whether you are beginning to develop an alcohol problem:

- You need to have a drink to hand.

- You need to drink every day.

- You become angry or defensive if others comment on your drinking.

- You have accidents and injure yourself through drinking.

- You make drinking a top priority, for instance at the expense of work or exercise.

- You get into trouble at work or with the law through, for example, drink-driving.

- You have to drink more and more to feel the effects of alcohol.

- You feel sick, have the shakes or start sweating in the middle of the night or in the morning.

To help reduce your drinking, consider the following:

- Record how much you drink every day to get a true picture of how much alcohol you consume.

- Avoid situations where you are likely to drink too much. If you are invited to an occasion where drink will flow, arrive late and leave early.

- Avoid the company of people you normally have heavy drinking sessions with.

- Drink slowly to make your drink last longer.

- Drink smaller measures of alcohol.

- Tell family and friends that you want to cut down so they can encourage you and back you up.

- If you don't want to tell others that you feel you drink too much, tell them you want to lose weight or that you are on antibiotics and not allowed to drink.

- If you can't cope by yourself, get outside help. (*See Useful Addresses, page 166.*)

Letting your mind run away with you

When stress has accumulated, your mind can be racing around like a driverless bus that is careering down a winding hillside. Your thoughts are constantly buzzing with what needs doing next, what you haven't achieved today and what is due to be added to your load tomorrow and the day after. How will you ever be able to get it all done, let alone get it done to your usual standards or get it done on time? While all these thoughts keep darting around in your mind, it can become impossible to switch off and sleep at night. As a consequence, you feel shattered and below par the next morning, which makes you even more stressed.

The effects of a driverless-bus mind can include some or all of the following:

- 'Freezing' – you can't do anything at all any more.

- Procrastination – you don't know where to start, so you put off starting anything at all and only a deadline will make you sprint into action.

- Inefficient hectic activity – you pick up lots of things but don't complete any.

- You become unbearable to live with – everything and everyone seems to add to your stress.

Whatever your stress reactions, the first thing to realise is that you are the driver of the bus, not a passenger, so get back into the driver's seat! It is your responsibility to run your mind, and it is your responsibility to keep it off the pavement so that no one else gets hurt.

To get a grip on your thought processes, do the following:

- Stop doing whatever you are doing and sit down.

- With your eyes closed, say to yourself: 'I am stopping this pandemonium *right now* and coming to my senses.' Say this to yourself again and again, with emphasis, until you can feel your thought processes slow down. (You have now stepped on the brake and pulled on the handbrake of your bus. The road is now flat in front of you, but you have run out of petrol.)

- Now say to yourself: 'I am starting to sort out this stress situation *right now*, calmly and efficiently.' (You have just turned round and taken control of the passengers behind you who are moaning that there is a hold-up.)

- Are there any tasks that someone has piled onto you that overburden you? Or, worse, any that you have piled onto yourself? Get on the phone *now* and cancel or postpone anything that is not strictly a priority. Do this before you do anything else. (You have just asked the passengers to get out of the bus and push it. More moaning!)

- Admit to yourself that this is all too much for you and you need to get some help. Are you worried that it 'doesn't count' unless you do everything yourself? Be aware that *no one* can do *everything* themselves. (As the driver of your bus, you will need to stay in control, so stay in the driver's seat. You cannot run without petrol and you cannot push the bus by yourself. It's OK to ask the passengers to help. The priority now is to get some petrol. The passengers are still moaning as they are pushing the bus. Never mind ...)

- Start planning how you are going to resolve your stressful situation and act on it *now*. (You just got your map out and found the quickest way to the service station where you can put some petrol in your tank.)

- Take a break. Once the worst is over and the most important things have been done, *stop*, even though there is more to do. Think whether it's really necessary to do all the other things. Cancel more things if you can. Have a few early nights to recover. (You have just part-refuelled but you haven't enough money for a full tank, so you have to think how far you can get on half a tank. Some of the passengers will have to take a train. You can't carry everyone to their destination.)

- Make sure in future that you have enough time to do all the tasks you agree to take on. (Next time, set off with a tank full of petrol.)

If you use the bus imagery in this way to ensure that you do not carry unnecessary loads in your life, soon your bus will become a nice convertible with power steering which you can handle easily and effortlessly!

Food for thought

Are you a square peg in a round hole?

Considering that we spend a great proportion of our waking hours at work, it is clearly important to make sure you like the work you do. It is not only an excessive workload that can create stress, but also being bored, not getting on with colleagues or the boss, or even feeling alone if you work for yourself.

Please answer the following questions, even if you are working on your own from home.

1. Are you using skills at work that correspond with your strong points?

2. Do you like at least 80 per cent of the work you do?

3. Do you get on with the majority of people who work with you/with whom you have to deal on a daily basis?

4. Do you find your work stimulating most of the time?

5. Is there scope for personal and professional development in what you do?

6. Are you being paid an acceptable amount for what you do? Do you earn an acceptable amount from the business you are running?

7. Is your work environment generally supportive of you? Do you get back-up from your family and friends in your work?

8. Do you feel lonely at work?

9. Do you feel appreciated at work? Do you appreciate your own achievements?

10. Do you have a clear concept of what is expected of you in your job? Do you have a clear concept of what you are doing in your job?

If you answered 'no' to any of the above questions, think about the following solutions:

1. If you are someone with strongly creative leanings who works in a repetitive, routine job, you can easily feel depressed and discontented. Make sure you take time for creative activities in the evenings or at weekends, or, better still, start looking for a job which allows you to express more of your creativity.

2. If not enough aspects of your work hold your attention in a positive way, you have either not chosen your job wisely or they didn't tell you the truth at the interview! In this case, you can either change jobs or pretend that you like

what you have to do. I'm not being sarcastic here – pretending to like an aspect of your work really has a stress-busting quality to it!

3. If you don't like the majority of people you have to deal with in your work, ask yourself whether it is you or them. Close your eyes and do the Screen Exercise (*see page 49*). If it is you, then you need to pull your socks up and deal with your negative attitude by doing the Respect Exercise (*see page 77*). If it's the others, you need to speak up for yourself, politely but firmly.

4. If your work is truly boring, is there anything you can do to make it more interesting? If you are required to sit around a lot of the time, can you read something? Can you learn something new? Do a bit of stretching or exercising? Practise one of the exercises in this section? Read the job opportunities section in the paper to find another job? It's action time! Self-pity won't get you anywhere.

5. A job is great as long as it feels comfortable while also stretching you. If you start becoming dissatisfied because you can do the job standing on your head, check out whether you can progress within the company. If this is not possible, make sure your time outside work holds some rewards and challenges – or change jobs!

6. Good work should be rewarded by just pay. If you feel very happy doing your work, if you feel appreciated and accepted, it is perfectly OK to do the work with little or even no pay. If you feel resentful about your low pay, however, don't let it fester. This needs sorting out; you owe it to yourself. If you are self-employed, invest time and effort into researching how you can make your business more profitable.

7. Are you the only one who is working while everyone else is making excuses and skiving off? Don't boil silently inside, speak to the person concerned, and if you don't get any joy there, speak to your boss. If your boss is

unsupportive or makes empty promises, start looking for another job. If your family is unsupportive, get everyone together for a pow-wow and tackle the issue. Can you find a way in which you can support each other?

8. You may think that working on your own is better because you don't have any company politics to contend with. This is true, but it can also be very lonely when you work without anyone else around. Make sure you interrupt your working day by having breaks that bring you into contact with other people. It is actually important to see someone and have a conversation face to face. It is not enough to just speak to someone over the phone or via e-mail. Having a relaxed face-to-face conversation with someone else reduces stress levels when you work on your own.

9. It is important to get positive feedback from your boss. If you feel you have done good work that has gone unrecognised, raise the issue with your superior. Explain what you have achieved and ask for your boss's comments. Blowing your own trumpet is OK as long as you point out your achievement to get recognition rather than to boast. When you are working for yourself, take some time out in the evening to establish what you have achieved during the day and give yourself a pat on the back.

10. Nothing is worse than feeling you are floundering through your allocated tasks, especially if the boss is unavailable or reluctant to give clear instructions. If you accept this situation without making yourself heard, you can easily end up taking a long time over a task and then getting the blame when things go wrong. Address this problem calmly and clearly in a sit-down meeting with your boss. Don't try and discuss this on the hoof while your boss is going out of the door – make a proper appointment. If nothing changes, look elsewhere. When you are working for yourself, make sure you set yourself clear objectives. If you need help with time management, read through the relevant section in this chapter (*see page 65*).

Giving a clear 'no' message

I'm always fascinated by what people mean when they say they have told someone 'no'. Time and time again it turns out that they did not give a clear message and were consequently lumbered with even more to do!

Unsuccessful stress management: saying 'no'

A recent client of mine was a highly-regarded university lecturer. She was already overburdened with a research project, preparations for a conference and her teaching assignments. When she heard that she would be expected to take on even more teaching work, she went to the head's office and, according to her, told him that she could not take on the extra work, only to find out a week later that she had been allocated additional teaching hours anyway. She felt exasperated, exhausted and at the end of her tether.

I asked her to tell me what exactly she had said to the head. It turned out that she had enumerated all the tasks she already had to cope with, including all the health problems she was struggling with at the moment.

Now you may think that surely the head should have understood that under these circumstances it would be unfair to give the lecturer more work, but clearly the message did not get through to him. The reason is that *the lecturer did not actually say 'no'*. Listing all the things you are already doing is not the same thing as saying 'no'. Listing all your current tasks can easily be dismissed as moaning but basically agreeing to a new work assignment.

Another sure way of *not* getting what you want is to ask questions such as 'Why can't we just stay at home and relax?' or 'Why are you so selfish?' or 'How would you feel if I did this?' Again, none of this will arrive as a clear message. Instead, you will probably hear that you are oversensitive, constantly moaning or a nag. It is much more effective to make a clear statement of what you want, for example 'I would like to stay home tonight and relax' or 'I'd appreciate it if you could turn the volume down' or

'I'd like you to stop staring at other men when we go out together.' These are clear instructions and leave no doubt about what you want. This in turn will reduce your stress levels enormously and help you feel more contented and in control.

Staying positive

I have often thought that an unpleasant or difficult life situation would be a lot easier to bear if someone could tell us reliably when it would end. Wouldn't it be reassuring to know that the rough patch your business was going through would all come right in 12 months' time? Or that if only you kept going with your sensible eating plan and kept taking your supplements, you would definitely have a great deal more energy in eight weeks' time? Or that you are guaranteed to meet Mr or Miss Right in two years' time?

The thing is, we don't know, and this is why it can be hard to hang on in there in difficult times. No wonder many people go to clairvoyants, hoping to get that certainty that it will all end well. I have done it myself quite a few times in the past when I wanted to be reassured that there was an end to a stressful situation. Once, when I had just put my house on the market, I consulted a clairvoyant who assured me the house would be sold, but not before the summer – a good six months on. I found that very helpful when four of my prospective buyers, one after the other, dropped out of buying my house. Having been told that the situation would be resolved, I just got on with my life. The house was finally sold in August.

What puzzled me for a long time, though, was the following question: if the future can be predicted, is there any point in striving for goals? If it is all out there, ready to happen, wouldn't it be easier just to wait and take what comes? Do we really have any part in shaping our destiny or is the die cast even before we are born? In other words, is there any point in making an effort to improve ourselves, our lives or our health? I personally have always planned new goals, worked towards them and eventually achieved them, often against all the odds.

So was it all in the stars anyway and I needn't have bothered to put in all the effort?

After thinking about this for a long time and discussing it with friends and colleagues, I have come to the conclusion that it is actually the other way round. Instead of telling you what destiny is holding in store for you, a clairvoyant is telling you what you have created for yourself so far.

There was a report in a Sunday paper recently about a healer helping a girl called Lara to walk again after she had been wheelchair-bound for years. The doctors had given up on her and she had given up on herself. Having been diagnosed as incurable, she could only think about things that depleted her energy. What the healer did was to make sure she changed her thought pattern about her condition. He instilled a new sense of purpose in her that made her focus on the energies she did possess and how she could harness and improve them. He taught her not only to stand up in a physical sense, but also to stand up for herself with friends who were demanding too much of her time. With the help of the healer, Lara began to make progress. She began to change her own reality for the better. Eventually she was able to stand up and walk again.

This may be an extreme example, but it is not an isolated one. People can achieve incredible feats when they are focused on a goal. And there is plenty of scientific evidence to show that this is all quite real. Lynne McTaggart has written a fascinating book called *The Field* in which she recounts the story of a group of frontier scientists who have been researching for decades into the effects our thoughts and intentions have on our environment, with amazing results. In the early 1970s, in the grip of the oil crisis, a handful of scientists, in the course of trying to find an alternative to petrol as vehicle fuel, accidentally stumbled on an element of quantum physics that seemingly had enormous potential. The Zero Point Field, a field of unimaginably large quantum energy in the space between things, an ocean of microscopic vibrations, seemed to hold the answer to many big questions. Here, in so-called 'dead' space, lay the very key to life itself – to cell communication, to DNA, to strange effects like extra-sensory perception or spiritual healing and even to that most elusive notion, the collective unconsciousness. It appears that our thoughts and intentions cause vibrations in the energy field around us which will then attract what we think about.

If this all sounds too 'new-agey' for you, consider the following. You have two people who are both single. One of them is very distressed by the fact, feeling depressed and hopeless and telling all their friends how miserable they feel without a partner. The other person lives each day in happy anticipation that their new partner is already on the way to them. Which one do you think is more likely to attract a suitable new partner? And which one is more likely to grab the next person who comes along, just to have any partner?

Or think of two people who are both being made redundant. One of them laments the fact all day long and indulges in feeling hard done by. The other one sits down immediately to update their CV, looks at how they can cut down on their spending and starts applying for a new job. Which one do you think will get through their time of unemployment more easily? Which do you think will come across better at interview? And which is more likely to come through this stressful period with their health intact? The answer is obvious.

The calmer you stay and the more optimistically you see into the future, the less stress you will experience. When you expect things to ultimately work out in your favour, you think and plan more constructively. Keeping hope alive will also spur you on to take the necessary action towards the resolution of your stressful situation.

There is an easy test to see whether your thoughts are geared towards the positive or the negative.

- Sit down for a moment and think about your stressful situation.
- Jot down your thoughts in the form of statements. If, for example, you are having problems with a work colleague, write down:

'This woman hates me.'
'I can't stand her.'
'We'll never get on.'

- Read your statements and check how they make you feel.

  If they make you feel down, they are unhelpful to you because they will block you from progressing towards an acceptable solution.

  If they make you feel hopeful, they are positive and you now need to follow them up with appropriate action.

You can basically look at life in two ways. You can take a difficult situation and generalise it ('This is what life is like!'), blame yourself for it ('I'm just no good!') and project it into the future ('This is the kind of thing that always happens to me!'). As a consequence of this attitude, you will classify anything good that happens to you or any success you have as a fluke which you cannot take credit for. Not a very happy way to live your life! In contrast to this unhelpful way of thinking, you can consider bad things as one-offs which help you learn new ways of coping. You don't go around blaming yourself for things that are not your fault, and when you make mistakes, you simply correct them or apologise for them and otherwise get on with your life. When things go right, you take credit for it, and you generally consider the world a good place to live in. The choice is yours. If you'd rather have a good time, go for a positive view!

Managing your time effectively

When the pace of life is hotting up to an uncomfortable level, it helps if you can organise the time you have more efficiently. This will ease the pressure and you will get more done.

To get a grip on your schedule, you will have to do a certain amount of planning. These are the basics:

- Define what you want to achieve. Be thorough and make a list of *all* your objectives.

- Arrange your projects into three groups of priority:
  1. Must be done today.
  2. Can wait until tomorrow.
  3. Long-term objective.

- Take your 'today' action list and arrange it in order of reluctance. Put the thing that you hate doing most at the top of the list.

- Do the thing you don't like doing *first*.

- As you work your way through the list, make sure you take little breaks, make sure you *breathe* while you are working and make sure you eat something (*see also page 121 about neglecting your life rhythm*). Drink plenty of good-quality water while you are working and don't put off going to the loo if you have to go.

- If you finish your 'today' list early, *stop working*. Don't make more work for yourself! Relax instead.

If there is a steady stream of things to do and you have a great number of long-term objectives, also consider the following:

- Have a year planner on the wall, whether you work in an office or at home. Mark on it the all-important projects and bigger events, including your holidays!

- Organise your timetable well ahead. You should know at least a month in advance what you need to do the following month.

- Allow ample time for tasks. Everything always takes longer and costs more than you think!

- Inform others of time limits in advance. This way everyone is clear about deadlines.

- Allow yourself breaks between projects. Don't finish one thing and get straight into the next. Taking breaks is important on a daily, weekly and monthly basis.

- It is OK to put off less important tasks until the next day (or week). If something keeps cropping up every week, it probably isn't that important. Consider dropping it.

- Have a tidy desk or work surface. Tidy things up every night before you finish work and only have those things on the desk that you need to do next.

- Do one thing at a time and do your best to finish it before you start on the next thing.

- Do important tasks when you are still fresh and energetic in the mornings and leave more routine tasks for later, or delegate them.

- Keep time free for yourself. Enter these free periods in your diary as you would with appointments.

- If you are busy with something important, let the answering machine take incoming calls.

- Think in terms of time available rather than number of tasks to be done. If you have three hours in the morning for certain tasks, think what you can reasonably achieve within this period of time.

- Allow regular time for social and family commitments. Make sure there is life after work!

- Remember that it is not necessary to carry out every single task to perfection.

- Remember that you are no good to anyone or yourself if you work yourself into the ground.

If you want to do well in life, your mental capacity needs to be fully at your disposal. Remembering clearly and making well-considered decisions hinge on your ability to concentrate and process incoming information in a detached and clear-headed way. If your emotions get in the way of your mental functioning, you need to tackle the emotional interference signals. The next chapter shows you how to do this.

CHAPTER FOUR

Coping with emotional upheaval

Emotions are great stuff when they are positive, but we tend to like them a lot less when they get in the way of what we want to do with our lives. They can assail us all of a sudden and for no apparent reason. Logically, we know we needn't be afraid of the job interview, but our emotions tell a different story. Our feelings can run away with us, and at times even run our lives. Sometimes they can be so close to the surface that our rational mind does not stand a chance – we *become* our emotions and feel out of control.

As we have seen, stress blocks our mental capabilities and a blocked mind creates performance which is below par. This in turn creates negative emotions. These form a memory trace of failure in the mind which then acts as a vicious circle – you begin to *expect* failure, which puts your emotions out of kilter even more.

Calming negative emotions is probably one of the more difficult things to do, but it is also one of the most rewarding. Life is so much easier when you are not weighed down by a riot of feelings but are able to take things in your stride.

This chapter is particularly relevant to you if you find yourself reacting in any of the following ways:

- You have become cynical about life and fear the worst is going to happen.

- You suffer from mood swings that are not connected to negative thoughts or memories.

- You feel overly aggressive, angry or weepy.

- You are very anxious or suffer from feelings of panic.

- You have lost your sense of humour.

- You feel down and depressed more often than not.

- You have been withdrawing from social life.

Emotional quick fixes

- Remember the last time you were worried about the future and how things resolved themselves then.

- If you have been labouring over something for a long time without getting results, you might as well let it go.

- Spend today pretending that you are the happiest person in the world.

- Speak to yourself in an encouraging way.

- Decide to believe that everything will work out fine.

- Pretend you don't care what others think of you and notice how many of your problems suddenly disappear.

- Look at the colour blue, which has a calming and relaxing effect on the emotions.

- Become sloppier when it comes to worrying.

- Give yourself praise for something you did well today and mean it!

- There is no law that says you have to become frantic when something doesn't work out. Refuse to panic when things go wrong.

Practical exercises

The Overload Soother

This is an excellent exercise to do, especially when your stress is accompanied by fear. In it, you cover a number of neurovascular points on your forehead and two others on the back of you head. Holding these points will help redirect the blood back to the forebrain. When we are stressed, the body switches into fight-or-flight mode and a large amount of blood leaves the brain to go to your arms and legs to help you fight or run fast. This, however, means that you cannot think very clearly because not enough oxygen is getting to your brain. By holding your hands over the neurovascular points, you calm your emotions so that panic can abate and you can feel back in control.

Please don't worry too much about exactly where these neurovascular points are. As you are using your entire hands, you will definitely cover the right areas.

- Put one hand across your forehead, just above the brows.

- Put the other hand over the back of your head to cover the two bumps at the base of your skull.

- Keep your hands in position until you feel calmer. This can take up to 15 minutes if your stress is particularly acute.

Under-8-Breathing

When emotions run high, your breathing will be fast and shallow, coming mainly from the chest area. Without enough oxygen reaching your brain, you will start to feel even more confused and anxious. This can result in the stress spiralling out of control and producing feelings of severe panic.

One way of controlling emotions is to focus on something else. Many people who suffer from nerves when they are getting on a plane find that as soon as someone is sitting next to them who feels very uncomfortable about flying, they forget about their own fears because they are busy helping the other person calm down.

As you won't always have someone else there to either calm you down or distract you, you need a method which allows you to distract yourself.

Before you do the main exercise, check the following:

- Sit quietly for about five minutes.

- Then look at a watch with a second hand and count how many times you breathe out over the period of one minute.

If you are relaxed and unstressed, your breathing rate will be *under* eight breaths a minute. If you are stressed, it will be anything from eight breaths upwards.

If your breathing is stressed even after five minutes' rest, you need to do the following exercise three times daily to get greater emotional relaxation.

If your breathing is below eight cycles a minute, you need the following exercise only when you are emotionally or otherwise stressed.

- Keep looking at the second hand of your watch while you breathe as follows:
  Breathe in slowly and deeply through your nose.
  Breathe out *slowly* through your mouth.

- At the same time, count each out-breath to see how many breaths you take in one minute.

- Continue the exercise until you have calmed your breathing to seven breaths a minute.

The Stress Tap

This is an exercise which is derived from Thought Field Therapy (TFT). TFT uses acupuncture points which are associated with stress responses.

By tapping these points while thinking about the stressful situation, you are helping your body release the stress response around the issue. This means that next time you think about your stress, your body does not react to it any more, so you can stay calm and relaxed.

The points to tap are as follows:

- at the start of the eyebrows

- under the eyes

- at the start of the collarbones

- under the arms

- on the side of one hand

Have a look at the diagram on page 73 to familiarise yourself with the position of the points, then do the exercise either sitting down or standing up.

- Tap each set of points about 10 to 20 times while at the same time *thinking about your stress*.

- You can tap quite quickly, but make sure you can clearly feel the tapping.

- When you tap the side of your hand, it is enough to do one hand only.

This exercise works very fast and for all sorts of stressful situations. If someone is getting on your nerves, go to the loo and tap, thinking about how annoying that person is. If you feel you can't cope, tap and think about your workload. If you have just had some bad news, tap and think about what you have just found out.

It is *very important* that you think about your stress while you are tapping the points. That way you give

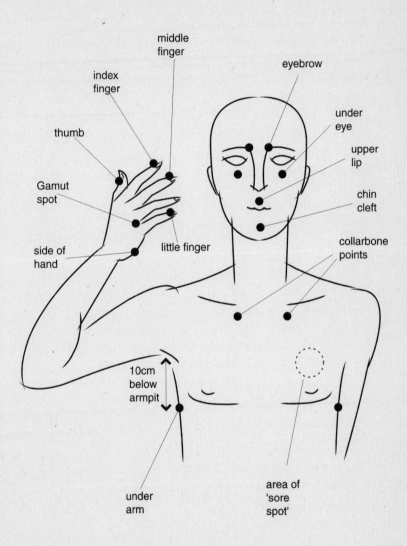

Figure 1. The Stress Tap

your body the information about which issue you would like to feel emotionally more relaxed.

Sometimes you may have to tap a few times a day for the same issue. That's OK. You may have to concentrate on different aspects of that issue. If, for example, you are overloaded with duties at home and at work, do one round of tapping while thinking about your tasks at home, then another round thinking about work at the office. You may also find it helpful to tap for different feelings you have about the overwork situation, such as 'I should cope better' and 'I resent my boss giving me so much to do.'

The Pyramid of Peace

This is another exercise which helps draw the mind away from stressful thoughts, anxiety and fear by making you focus intently on something quite different. In contrast to the Under-8-Breathing exercise, the Pyramid of Peace is suitable for night-time as well as daytime.

The exercise consists of visualising the four main geometric shapes contained within the structure of a pyramid – the oval, circle, square and triangle. It should be done sitting down or standing up. Imagine each shape being drawn seven times around your whole body while you are breathing as indicated. In the figure below, the dark lines represent in-breaths, the light lines out-breaths.

Oval

- Breathe in and draw one half of the oval from your head down to your feet.

- Now breathe out while you draw the other half from your feet up to your head.

- Repeat six times. Press a finger against your bed or chair on completing each round.

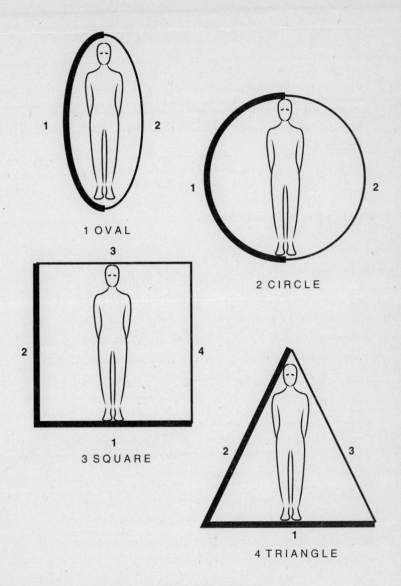

Figure 2. The Pyramid of Peace

Circle

- Breathe in while drawing the circle from your head down to your feet.

- Breathe out while drawing the other half of the circle from your feet up to your head.

- As a circle is bigger than an oval, your breaths should be deeper as you imagine drawing the circle in your mind.

- Repeat six times, counting each round by pressing a finger down on the bed or chair.

Square

- The in- and out-breaths are split into four counts now.

- Breathe in and draw the base line under your feet.

- Keep on breathing in and draw the right side of the square up to your head.

- Start breathing out and draw the top line of the square over your head.

- Finish breathing out while drawing the left side of the square down to the base line beneath your feet.

- Repeat until seven whole squares have been drawn. Count each completed square by pressing a finger down.

Triangle

- Breathe in and draw the base line under your feet.

- Keep breathing in and draw the line up your right side to the apex over your head.

- Now breathe out and draw the line from the apex down to the left side.

- Repeat until seven whole triangles have been drawn, pressing down a finger after each completed round.

The Respect Exercise

If you were a teacher and you had a classroom full of average and good students, with *one* youngster who was struggling, how would you help that less talented student to give their best so they can catch up with the others? There are three things that a good teacher would do: treat that student as an individual rather than comparing them with the others, encourage them, and praise them for what they *can* do. By doing those things, you are showing your student respect, and showing respect teaches self-respect. Without self-respect, there can be no respect for others. Without self-respect, there is constant stress.

The Respect Exercise comes in three steps. Although it takes all three to build up solid self-respect, even one step will help you a lot on your way.

Step 1: stop comparing yourself to others

You are an individual and you are unique. No one has gone through exactly the same experiences as you have and no one has exactly the same emotional make-up as you have. No one else can take your place in the world. There is something special you are meant to do with your life, and you need to get on with doing it rather than envying others or feeling sorry for yourself.

You may be unable to love or even like yourself at this stage, and that is OK. What is *not* OK is if you don't *respect* yourself.

Use the following affirmation every day for at least three weeks. Use it every morning and every evening – think it, say it, sing it, I don't care how you do it, just do it!

'I have a unique task to fulfil in life and I'm the only person who can do it.'

By using this positive thought, you acknowledge and respect that you are an individual who needs to seek individual solutions in order to find an individual way of living a happy and stress-free life.

Step 2: encourage yourself

Yes, I know, you shouldn't have to do this all by yourself, and really your parents should have done it for you when you were little, but this is still no excuse for not doing it for yourself now. If you feel quite obstinate about it and try and hide behind the excuse that you don't know *how* to encourage yourself, imagine what you would say to a very good friend who was in your stressful situation. How would you encourage them? We can often find the words to encourage others when we fail to encourage ourselves.

Thinking briefly about your current stress, say something encouraging and supportive to yourself, for example 'I can do this!' or 'I can get through this!' or 'One day at a time. I'm doing well!' Say or think your encouragement, just like your affirmation, in the morning and in the evening every day for at least three weeks. Also, say it every time you feel overwhelmed by stressful thoughts. Encouraging yourself will keep you going until a positive solution to your stress can be found.

Step 3: praise yourself for what you are doing well

Why is it that only bad news travels fast, even in our heads? How come many of us could write, within minutes, a substantial list of our weaknesses, faults and physical shortcomings, but struggle to write down five good things about ourselves? Maybe it is false modesty that prevents us from admitting that we have positive traits, or maybe our culture encourages us to concentrate on the negative sides of ourselves because those are the ones that need improving. Instead try the following:

- In one minute, write down as many of your strengths and positive traits of character as you can. (You won't have to show the list to anyone else, so don't be shy!)

How many did you get? Anything under five, take another minute to think a bit more. If you can't find any more positive points about yourself, ask a friend. You should be able to come up with around 10 positive traits about yourself within a minute. This shows that you have a good opinion of yourself, and that is important. If *you* can't appreciate yourself, how can others?

- Now take this little exercise one step further. Think about your stressful situation and this time, rather than giving yourself a hard time over not doing certain things well enough, look at how your strong points help you to deal with it. Really look closely. Just because you haven't resolved a stressful situation yet doesn't mean you haven't done well.

Here is a little list of positive characteristics that people find helpful when under stress. Do you display any of the following qualities?

resourceful	inventive	helpful	tenacious
patient	flexible	reliable	resilient
loyal	diplomatic	optimistic	determined
understanding	co-operative	focused	hardworking

Does your tenacity help you to hang on in there when other people would have given up? Does your flexibility or inventiveness allow you to cope better than if you were more rigid and unimaginative? Have you achieved a lot, considering the severity of the situation?

Add a third sentence to your step 1 and 2 sentences, something like:

'I'm glad I'm so [insert your strong quality]. This is really helpful in this stressful situation.'

If you cannot find anything good to say about yourself, imagine someone else having to cope with your situation and dealing with it in the same way you do. Now can you find something good to say about that person's handling of the situation? If so, well done. If not, please don't worry. Just get on with steps 1 and 2 for the time being and step 3 will become possible a bit later. Simply try it again in a week or two and you might surprise yourself. If you can find even one good aspect about yourself to acknowledge, that will be a great step forward on the road to self-respect.

As your self-respect improves, you will start to look at people around you with different eyes. As you are looking for the good and strong in yourself, so you will begin to appreciate the positive aspects of others. Your shift in perception will also make you act more confidently and calmly, and these are the very qualities that will help you resolve problems more easily.

A protective shield

You may feel that you are quite positive but that negative energies from those around you stress you during the course of the day. The following exercise can prevent unwanted influences from affecting you. In order to shield yourself, you simply use your imagination to build a safe space around you. This may sound unbelievable, but there is in fact scientific evidence that it actually works. In her book *The Field*, Lynne McTaggart describes the following experiment:

> Each participant in this experiment was linked up o a skin tension meter. One group was told to mentally shield themselves against attempts by two experimenters to raise their skin tension levels. A control group was also told that experimenters would try to raise their skin tension levels, but without being instructed to shield themselves mentally against this influence. At the end of the experiment, the control group showed significantly more physical effects than those participants who had shielded themselves. Mental shielding had been able to rebut outside influence.

You can shield yourself too. Use the following example as a guideline but feel free to alter it so it fits in with your personal preferences.

- Close your eyes.

- Imagine yourself standing in a golden circle. A strong white light flows from above your head all the way around you, like a big spotlight, and reaches down to your golden circle.

- Imagine that the white light lets you see clearly everything around you but repels all negativity coming from the outside. Negative thoughts, feelings and actions from your environment are simply reflected back to the sender as they bounce off your protective shield.

Emotional self-sabotage

Life can be difficult enough without you adding to it with unhelpful attitudes and habits. A simple way of finding out whether you are tripping yourself up is to check whether any of the following makes you feel uptight or moody:

- sitting down and not doing anything
- starting on one particular train of thought
- speaking to someone else about a problem you have
- thinking about yourself and how you are doing in life
- thinking about people close to you

If any of the above makes you feel stressed, chances are that you lack self-respect or you lack respect for others. If you end up feeling bad-tempered or tense, you clearly have some habitual thought processes that don't work *for* you but *against* you.

Blaming and generalising

Habitual negative thoughts normally involve blaming and generalising and fall into one of three categories:

Category 1: blaming yourself

Here you indulge in disrespectful thoughts about yourself by slagging yourself off for not having achieved what you should achieve or for being unlikely to achieve anything in the future. These disrespectful thoughts about yourself are there all the time, but they are normally pushed into the background while you are busy. Once you sit down and there is nothing to distract you, they will come to the fore, and that is why your mood deteriorates. If you are already in a stressful situation, your negative attitude towards yourself will make matters worse. You will feel terrible about yourself, put yourself down and become discouraged, listless and depressed – not a good place to be if you want to cope with stress!

The reason why these self-denigrating thoughts can be so tenacious is usually because someone or something in the past has taught you to think like that. It often only takes one critical failure or one over-demanding person for you to start thinking that you are not good enough. Even years later, this old message can stay as strong and discouraging as it was on the day when you first experienced it.

So what can you do if the past still has a hold over you?

■ Admit that you are not perfect and never will be and congratulate yourself on having joined the human race at long last. It takes a lot of pressure off when you stop harassing yourself.

■ Decide to do the best you can in life, but not more.

■ Acknowledge that you have done your best.

■ When you need help, admit it and make sure you ask for it.

Category 2: assuming that others will let you down

Being disrespectful towards others is every bit as unhelpful as being disrespectful towards yourself. It is of course true that other people's actions can cause us considerable distress, embarrassment or pain. If this pain overwhelms us so that we feel our daily life is compromised by it, then we will have to address this unacceptable behaviour. If we are in a stressful situation and expected help but didn't get it, we need to ask ourselves why that is.

In this case the automatic habitual and highly emotional answer is usually 'Because X doesn't care!' But hang on a moment – is this really true? Did you clearly say that you needed help? Or did you *expect* the other person to know automatically that you needed support? What appears obvious to you may not be at all obvious to someone else, so please don't sulk because they didn't read your mind. It is your responsibility as an adult to *ask* for what you need, and to ask clearly. Statements like 'You are not very supportive' or 'Thanks a lot for letting me do XYZ all by myself' and going all moody do not qualify as asking for help. Equally unhelpful, in fact downright useless is telling *others* how self-centred they are. That is definitely not going to change things for the better!

What will get results is a straight request expressed in a polite way. Say, for example, 'This bag is too heavy for me. Can you please take it off me?' or 'I feel really tired at the moment. Can you please go and pick up the children for me today?' Only if you have requested help in a direct way and got no support can you query the other person's willingness to help. If you do not make a clear request, you are sabotaging yourself and preventing the other person from getting it right.

If you feel yourself balking at having to make a direct request, you will need to check your attitude. What can you do when you find it difficult to ask for help?

- Start your request with the following opener: 'I find it very difficult to ask for help, but could you please …'

- Stop saying 'nothing' if someone asks you what the matter is.

- Be aware that many people need to be trained to be helpful. That goes for your partner as much as for your children and work colleagues. You'd better get cracking straight away, starting with the person who is most likely to agree to help.

Category 3: blaming life in general

Typical thoughts here are 'Life is unfair', 'I'm always unlucky', 'People are cruel' or 'Life is hard.' But any sweeping statements like these are bound to be incorrect. Life can of course be unfair at times, and certain people can be cruel a lot of the time, but nothing *always* happens, good or bad. And by immersing yourself in negative generalisations, you are shirking your personal responsibility to do something about your particular situation. If you maintain that life is stressful, then there seems little point in doing anything about it. If, however, a particular situation or even several situations are stressing at the moment, you can tackle them one by one to resolve them so you can gain greater peace of mind.

What can you do to leave behind the old habits of generalising and staying inactive?

- Add something to your generalisation. If you catch yourself thinking (or saying) 'Life is unfair,' add: 'But not always.'

- Check what the specific situation is that made you think or utter the generalisation. Where are you *right now* and what can you do about it?

- When you find yourself reciting a list of other events that prove that life is unfair, stop yourself and make a concerted effort to list all the things that happened in your life that *were* fair. This of course includes situations such as not preparing for an exam and failing it!

Putting up with the unbearable

If you are in a relationship that upsets you most of the time, you have a serious problem that needs resolving. If you are in a job where working conditions or the general atmosphere are unacceptable, it will start dominating your thoughts and emotions after a while. The same is true if you are single-handedly looking after ageing relatives without getting any support or if you are constantly expected to deal with a massive workload without receiving recognition or help.

The question you need to ask yourself is why, if the situation is that unbearable, are you still in it? Here are a few standard excuses:

- 'If I don't do it, it won't get done.'
- 'If I don't do it myself, it won't get done properly.'
- 'If I don't do it, I'm leaving someone else in the lurch.'
- 'If I stop doing it now, the other person won't understand. They expect me to keep on doing it because I've always done it.'
- 'If I stop doing it now, the other person will be offended/hurt, and I couldn't live with that.'
- 'If I don't keep doing it, I will feel I have failed.'
- 'If I don't keep doing it, I'm selfish.'
- 'It is a sign of weakness if you want to leave a difficult situation.'

It is of course very good to take your responsibilities seriously, to persevere with tasks that have been given to you or that you have chosen to undertake. It is laudable to be reliable and hardworking, but not if you destroy yourself and your emotional well-being in the process! If you do damage to yourself in the course of doing what you perceive as being your duty, nobody wins. What happens is that you manoeuvre yourself into illness and any people who rely on you are suddenly left without your help and without any warning.

One main reason why people stay in an unbearable situation is because they are ashamed to admit that they find the situation emotionally draining. Late at night, however, alone in bed, they can feel their own distaste and agony over their present circumstances. As these feelings are uncomfortable and they are ashamed of them, they clamp down on them and tell themselves they shouldn't feel like that. In this way, they are trying to make the negative feelings go away, but of course they won't. All that happens is another negative feeling is added – guilt. Guilt at having the negative feelings in the first place.

Feelings come from the subconscious level of your mind

and they are either there or they are not there. There is nothing in between. Just as your body can't be a little bit dead or a little bit pregnant, so your feelings are either there or not there. And they won't go away just because you don't want them to be there.

Disregarding your feelings and denying that a task has become an emotional burden shows that you have no self-respect, and that is every bit as bad as not having respect for others. Where did you learn to believe that your feelings don't count? More often than not, it is from the person who is now demanding you do the impossible for them – most often a parent or someone very like one of your parents.

Ignoring unpleasant emotions isn't the answer. The only way forward is to acknowledge them and take action to change your circumstances in such a way that your emotional stress load is lightened.

But now you often encounter another obstacle – your expectation of other people's adverse reactions. What will they say if you tell them you can't go on doing what you have been doing? How will they react? Will they still like you? What will the neighbours/friends/family say?

In 90 per cent of cases, people will turn out to be much more understanding than you thought, provided you state your case clearly and politely. Some may even apologise to you for having lumbered you with the load. They may have been unaware how difficult your situation had become and may be happy to help you find a different solution.

The other 10 per cent of people will try and keep you doing what you have always done because it suits them better. They may try to emotionally blackmail you by playing on your inner fears, namely that you are letting them down and that you are being selfish if you don't continue bearing the unbearable. But stop and think for a moment – who is really the selfish person here? If *you* were told by someone that what they were doing for you made them feel distressed and overburdened, would *you* think it was right to continue asking them to do it? Stop applying double standards. If something would not be fair for *you* to do, then it is also not fair if *others* treat *you* like that. Stop putting everyone else before yourself or you will become a slave to your inability to respect yourself. Of course there is nothing wrong with being helpful and dedicated, but there is something very wrong if you are riding roughshod over your own emotions and letting other people be disrespectful towards you.

If you find yourself in a situation that makes you unhappy, you will need to tackle it sooner or later, so you might as well do something about it right now.

- Admit to yourself that you are unhappy and tell yourself that it is OK to feel that way.

- Decide whether you need to leave your current situation altogether or whether you can modify it to make it more bearable.

- Set up a meeting with the people who are involved in your stressful situation.

- Be clear what it is you want. Get your facts straight and practise in front of the mirror what you want to say.

- In the meeting, be as calm as you can and say politely but clearly what you want.

- There are two exceptions to the above. One is if you are with someone who has violent tendencies. In that case, don't negotiate. Walk out and don't go back. You are responsible for your own safety. The other case is if you have talked to the person concerned, and you have done so politely and clearly on several previous occasions without getting results. If you have given someone a second and a third chance, you owe it to yourself to finally leave that situation.

Food for thought

Relationships: shockers or shock-absorbers?

There is no doubt that a supportive network of family and friends can help significantly towards overcoming a stressful episode in your life. Even if you have only *one* relative or friend who backs you up when things get tough, it can give you the vital bit of extra energy to cope better. We can deal with anything more easily if we feel understood and supported.

Ideally, your support team comes from your own family. But not every family will pull together when one of its members needs help. Some families become fragmented over a stressful situation. In yet other families, it is the children who act as shock-absorbers for problems that the parents are experiencing.

A family becomes dysfunctional when children become their parents' parents instead of remaining their parents' children. If you think of a family as a hierarchical system where the older generation looks after the younger one by passing down their knowledge, support and encouragement, then the new generation can do the same in turn for their own children. If, however, the older generation is still busy trying to cope with the shortfall of love and understanding from *their* parents, then they will be too preoccupied with their own stress to pay appropriate attention to their children's needs. This creates tension not just between parents and children, but also between the parents themselves, even if only one parent has suffered from emotional neglect by their parents. When this is the case, a child will often try to be what they think their unhappy parent wants them to be. Or the child will try to do what they think will help the parent become happy. This can sometimes go on for the rest of that child's life and can extend way past the unhappy parent's lifetime. The child's focus of attention remains directed backwards onto the mother or father rather than forwards towards their own partner and/or children who in turn are shortchanged of support and affection.

In a well-functioning family, the children can lean on their parents until they are old enough and strong enough to stand by themselves. This means that their own children can lean on them later on in life. When one or both parents are not available for their children to lean on, the children are often inclined to look after their parents so that eventually the parents lean on the children. This is a terrible burden for a child to carry and such children often pay a high price for it later on in life. They can become strongly duty-driven and over-responsible without heeding their own needs. This is because they never had the luxury of having their own needs met when they were little. They took on a protective and caring function as children and simply don't know how to lay down this load and look after themselves.

There are many reasons why a person becomes unavailable for their child or partner. A daughter who as a child has been used by her mother as confidante and support because the father was not available emotionally to the mother won't feel that her own worries are worth mentioning in view of the mother's (perceived) greater needs. This daughter may well take a dim view of men and later treat her own husband and son with less love than they deserve. On one level, she is still defending her mother against her father. This can lead to her jeopardising her own marriage and raising her son to feel unsupported and like a second-class citizen. This in turn lowers the son's chances of making a future relationship work and giving support to a partner and children.

There is nothing we can do about our parents' history, but we can certainly make sure that the buck stops with us. Here are some questions you may want to ask yourself to find out whether you are still entangled in your childhood:

- Are you over 30 years old and still complaining about your parents?

- Do you find yourself remembering childhood memories to do with your parents and feeling hurt or resentful about them?

- Are you behaving in a way that you always hated in your mother or father?

- Are you convinced your parents never did anything right for you?

- Do you still engage in inner arguments with your parents even though they are no longer alive?

- Do you find it difficult to show love to your partner and/or children?

Any of this behaviour is a sign that you are not yet fully disengaged from your childhood. And while you are caught up in the past, you are unavailable to either a partner or your children. You are also unavailable to yourself. You are still waiting for your parents to tell you that you are the best thing that ever happened to them. This is a terrible thing to have to wait for if your parents themselves are still waiting for this very same message from *their* parents. Meanwhile, your partner and children have to run on empty because you are engaged in the past.

The way forward from here is to get some professional help with overcoming the childhood events that keep you prisoner in the past. Once you embark on therapy, lots of your present stresses will begin to disappear and your relationships with your own family will take a turn for the better. In some cases, this can mean having to leave an unsuitable partner; in other cases it can save a relationship and make it stronger. But even if your relationship with your partner ends as a result of you going through therapy, you will be more of a parent to your children by looking after yourself rather than making your children feel they have to look after you. Once you have left the entanglements with your own childhood behind, you can fully turn to your children and give them the support they deserve. And the best thing is that you are now also more likely to find a partner who appreciates and loves you and with whom you can be happy.

Successful stress management: impatience with children

Kim (26) loved her children but felt she couldn't cope with them. 'I feel so bad,' she reported. 'I always seem to scream at them, even over small things. I know I shouldn't do it, but I can't stop myself. And the worst thing is that I feel I'm just like my mother, and I have always sworn I would do things differently with my children.' Kim felt racked with guilt for being so harsh not just with the children, but also with her husband. She blamed herself for her three-year-old boy having developed a stutter. She felt depressed and at the end of her tether.

In her hypnotherapy sessions, it turned out that Kim's parents had had an unhappy marriage, with the father being monosyllabic and the mother resenting the father's frequent absences from home. When he finally turned up late at night, the mother would yell accusations at him at the top of her voice, shouting herself into a frenzy which was made worse by the father never responding. While all this was going on, Kim and her two sisters were anxiously listening to the commotion going on downstairs. The following day, her mother would complain to the girls about their father.

What Kim had learnt during her childhood was that men were unreliable and left you in the lurch once you had children, and that children were a nuisance. Even though she had not been consciously aware of holding those beliefs, they had nevertheless directed her behaviour.

In her sessions, Kim learnt to relax and to breathe more deeply, and after working through some of her key memories, she felt much more comfortable being around her children. She could enjoy being a mother without getting stressed out about it. Another positive side-effect was that she was able to deal more confidently with the children, which in turn helped them become calmer and better behaved.

Boundaries and rules

Were you brought up with the instruction of putting everyone else first and yourself last? Maybe it was not expressed in quite such a categorical manner, but you understood intuitively that it was 'wrong' to put yourself first.

Were you given to understand that people in authority, members of the medical profession or those with a better education or job than you are always right?

Have you been taught that there is only ever *one* right way of doing things and that your way is normally the wrong one unless you do as you are told?

Have you ever made a rule of your own in life or are you constantly living according to other people's rules?

In order for us to live together in comparative harmony, there has to be a certain consensus of how we relate to one another. We need communal rules that allow for the smooth exchange of services that we can render one another. For example, we need to have an agreed currency and modes of payment that we all share. We need a set of rules that we live by, commonly known as the law, to determine what can or cannot be done within a community. These laws may exist in writing or may be traditional unspoken laws that we strive to keep to in order to prevent injustice or disorder. But however they are laid down, there have to be rules and boundaries so that a community can live together peacefully and in an orderly fashion.

Most rules, written or unwritten, place a great emphasis on the greater good of the community, that is your family, neighbours, friends or strangers. If everyone were to do whatever they felt like and just looked out for themselves, we would soon have chaos. If you have ever driven a car in a big city in India, you will have witnessed this chaos. Someone decides to have a chat with a shopkeeper, so they stop their car in the middle of the road. Someone else wants to buy something at a stall by the roadside and simply leaves their car parked in the road while they spend a good hour haggling over the price of the goods. In the meantime, horns are hooting and no one else can get past. The angry shouting or hooting may raise a dismissive wave of the hand from the person blocking the road, but certainly does not speed up clearing a way through.

While the Far East can cope with this lawlessness, we in the West seem to be happier with clearer outlines and boundaries as to how far we can inconvenience the next person. Our society is strongly governed by guilt, and maybe it is this that makes us create lots of rules and laws which are meant to prevent us from becoming guilty. At the same time, there is a deeply ingrained sense of right and wrong in us which governs our daily lives. It is this that creates a lot of stress.

How does this happen? For one thing, there is the concept

of being a good person if you help others. So if your work colleagues cannot cope with their duties, you need to help them out. If you want to be a good daughter, you spend every weekend with your ageing parents. If you want to be a good citizen, you give to charity, you help out your neighbour and you don't block someone else's driveway (or the entire road) with your car. Getting all these things right will give you the reward of feeling good about yourself. Being supportive and caring is of course excellent and it has been shown that communities which operate on this principle work together harmoniously, with a much lower risk of heart disease and other serious illnesses. Positive communication and a close-knit social network make for a good atmosphere and for good health.

But what happens if someone is exploiting that rule? Instead of helping others and being helped in turn, some people will claim help for themselves without ever being there for others. Some take advantage of others without giving back. Others rest on their rights of being the elders and therefore able to demand anything they like. And others have a plain double standard: others have to help them, but they don't have to help others. What do you do now? How do you deal with these people?

Oddly enough, we don't seem to have any rules to cover these circumstances. Nothing in our interhuman rules and regulations allows for people who shirk their responsibilities or make unreasonable demands on others. Our sense of guilt still dictates that we serve these people, even though everything within us might rebel. But if we were to refuse, we would be as 'bad' as they are. We would have come down to their level.

This rule of having to help at all costs can cause havoc if it is applied without boundaries. This is especially true within families. If a wife refuses to seek outside help for a phobia and obliges her husband and children to do everything for her, she causes unfair stress on her family. This distressing state of affairs will only come to an end when someone puts their foot down and refuses to help out until the wife seeks help. Similarly, if a child runs rings around the parents, being demanding, noisy and uncooperative, this will cause them great stress. Unless they take a firmer stand and set clear boundaries for the child, neither they nor their child will be able to thrive and enjoy each other. In this context, it is a big mistake to exempt children with a disability from having to observe boundaries. Learning to stick to a set of rules which get everyone to do their share of chores within the family helps children to fit in better within the community outside the family.

What we often fail to teach our children is that no one is automatically right because they hold a certain position or are of a particular age or gender. By taking a neighbour's or teacher's word as gospel, we may not do justice to our child's ability to tell us what happened. However, giving in to our child's wishes to the detriment of our own well-being is equally unfair. We need to teach our children that there needs to be give and take in relationships with others.

Think back to what you learnt as a child and then take a moment to define the rules you *live by* (not the ones you theoretically hold to be true!). Do your personal rules allow you to draw boundaries that protect you from unreasonable demands? Or do they end up as self-sabotage? Are you trying to be good without expecting others to pull their weight? Does your attitude allow others to take advantage of you? Are you, more often than not, the one who is left holding the baby?

Although it is not easy to go against inherited rules, it can be done and it works very well.

Successful stress management: re-educating the family

Heather (53) was a participant on one of my courses. We were having a group discussion about things that we found stressful and several women in the group reported that they had always felt that they did not have enough time for themselves in their role as mother and wife. Without exception, they had all learnt from their own mothers that the family came first. Heather, too, had been brought up in this tradition but had decided to break out. She taught her family how to use the washing machine and explained to them that they would each need to do their own washing and ironing as she couldn't do everything on her own any more.

'I had expected a great deal of resistance,' Heather explained, 'but it really wasn't that bad, although I felt very guilty for making these demands on my family. But after a few weeks everyone was doing their own washing and ironing, and it wasn't a problem at all.'

Using anger constructively

Stress can bring out the worst in us and in some people it brings out anger. They are already tense and irritable, and then one more thing happens and they explode. If that one more thing is you coming in the door and asking a question, you will get it. This may mean being shouted at, having a sarcastic remark thrown in your direction or being studiously ignored. None of these reactions are a pleasant experience …

If you yourself are someone who flies off the handle when you are stressed, you may well be aware of what you are doing but be unable to stop yourself. Once the stress build-up has gathered a certain momentum, it takes over and you feel unable to stem the angry outburst. Most people feel really bad afterwards and apologise to their 'victims', but there are only so many anger tantrums you can get away with before you become seriously unpopular, no matter how regularly you apologise.

Anger is the result of fear. You are either afraid of losing control over a situation or you feel you have already lost control. You may be worried that you will get it in the neck if you don't meet your deadline, or be afraid that others will let you down, which will then reflect negatively on *your* reputation. You may be afraid of others not respecting you or even defying you, so you make unpleasant sarcastic remarks or ignore them. Even though you are not shouting, these reactions are still expressions of anger.

If you have a short fuse, use any of the following exercises to help you keep your cool.

The anger room

- Close your eyes and imagine that you are in a room with many shelves and several big tables, all of which are loaded with china, glasses and knick-knacks.
- Imagine getting hold of a baseball bat and starting to demolish absolutely everything in the room, including the shelves and tables.
- Don't stop until you have smashed everything to smithereens.

This exercise is particularly good if you feel frustrated but there is nothing you can do about your situation. You may have been made redundant and finding it hard to find a new job or your children may be going through a phase where they drive you crazy. Use the Anger Room to let off steam – you will feel better for it and you will be able to speak more calmly to your children afterwards.

Count to 10

Yes, I know, that old chestnut, but it does work. When you feel yourself building up to an explosion:

- Don't say anything.
- Count to 10 in your mind – and count slowly!
- Take a deep breath before you start speaking.
- Speak slowly and in a low voice. That will help you keep your cool.

Dealing with angry people

When you are on the receiving end of an angry outburst, be aware that you do not have to accept this kind of behaviour.

   If the angry person is your boss, it can be particularly

hard to stomach it, especially when you feel your job is on the line if you answer back. You feel intimidated by the implied or open criticism coming your way in this rude manner, and it is very tempting to immediately agree and apologise. This is a good way of getting your critic off your back quickly, but it doesn't do a lot for your self-esteem. You are likely to walk off seething and feeling sorry for yourself and spend the next week stewing and scheming how to get back at the other person.

Shouting back is of course an option and it will certainly allow you to let off steam, but it is not a very constructive way of dealing with someone else's angry outburst.

No matter whether the shouter is your boss or your mother, there are simpler and less energy-consuming ways of countering them:

- Say in a low voice, 'I'll come back when you feel calmer.' Then leave the room, closing the door behind you quietly.

- If the outburst happens over the phone, say quietly, 'Give me a ring back when you feel calmer.' Then hang up.

On either occasion, it is perfectly OK to talk over the other person. Don't be worried that they won't hear you because you are speaking quietly. Somehow people do pick up what you say, even while they themselves are shouting.

If someone is attacking you with sarcastic remarks:

- Repeat what they just said to you in a factual tone of voice, for example:

  Boss (in a sarcastic tone): 'I found your "so-called" report on my desk this morning!'
  You (in a level voice): 'You found my so-called report on your desk this morning.'

- Now wait. Don't say anything more.

By feeding back what the person has just said to you, you bring it home to them how they are speaking to you, and that often stops them in their tracks. You might even get an apology out of them!

Another way of feeding back to the angry person is to acknowledge their sarcasm.

- *You:* 'You sound sarcastic. Is there a reason for this?'
- Now wait. Don't say anything more.

This way, you are preserving your energy and letting the other person correct their own behaviour. If they continue being nasty or sarcastic, get up and tell them to let you know when they want to discuss matters in a calmer way with you.

Angry words or nasty criticism will not change people's behaviour, just make them dislike you more and become less co-operative. If you have reason to criticise, make sure you do it in a factual way that is mainly positive and encouraging. Let us say a teenage member of your family has tidied up their mess in the living room, but they haven't done it very well, and they certainly haven't done it as well as you could have done. You can now have a fit of anger or you can see this as a starting-point for greater co-operation. In other words, you can now have a thoroughly bad time or a reasonably OK time. It's really up to you. Which would you prefer?

The quickest way to have a reasonably good time is to say 'Thank you!' and leave it at that.

To ensure further co-operation, say, 'Thank you. Your tidying up has really helped me.'

Encouragement and praise will always win the day because it makes others feel valued and appreciated. So if you really *have* to criticise, couch it as positive feedback. 'You've done a great job here. Well done!

Could you just pick up your socks from behind the sofa and put them in the laundry basket? Brilliant. Thanks.'

Your teenager will still think you are an embarrassing presence and too uncool for words, but they have done the job you wanted them to do, so what the hell …

Contagious moods

While it is true to say that we often generate our own stress by taking a negative view of a situation or by neglecting to set clear boundaries that help preserve the space and respect we need, we are of course not immune to other people's moods and attitudes.

Anyone who has ever worked or travelled in a group will know how one moody person can mar the atmosphere for the whole group – if you let them. What tends to happen is that everyone begins to physically move away from the surly person or tries to keep the greatest possible distance from them. This can be very difficult when the moody person is your boss or a close family member!

There are many different ways in which someone can express their moodiness. Some people clam up and look sulky, others complain about everything and everyone, or criticise you endlessly. Depending on your disposition, you either become moody yourself or stressed out by the other person's bad mood. Some people can stand the presence of a sulky person better than others, but after a while most people are adversely affected.

Why is it so difficult to remain immune to other people's moods? I think there are two main reasons. One is that we take someone else's bad mood personally. We immediately start searching for something we may have said or done that could have upset them. This can lead to the most outlandish assumptions of what we might have done wrong. But they are only assumptions and could be totally wrong. One way out of the dilemma would be to simply ask what the matter is, but once we have tacitly assumed responsibility for the other person's bad mood, we don't really want to hear the answer, so now there are *two* people who won't talk!

The other reason why we are affected by someone else's bad mood can be that we feel personally responsible for restoring their good humour, either because we can't stand the tense atmosphere any more or because we think we may be the cause of their upset. We then start doing things to please the other person, trying to cheer them up or to distract them to jolt them out of their emotional black hole. This can work, but often it doesn't. So what do you do now?

Please note: There is no law that says you have to be connected with an umbilical cord to someone else's emotions. Please read this sentence slowly at least three times and really think about it. You may in the past have *believed* that your emotions are dependent on how those around you feel, but that doesn't mean it is true. Your emotions can be quite sepa-rate from other people's if you want them to be. You can *decide* to be emotionally detached from others.

This is a matter of taking responsibility. You need to take responsibility for your emotions and other people need to be responsible for theirs. If you have done something to upset another person, it is their responsibility to let you know what it is. This way you are enabled to assess whether you need to set something right or whether you need to apologise. If the other person does not wish to reveal what you have done to upset them, it does *not* become your responsibility to find out, although I would recommend that you at least ask once whether you have done anything to upset them. There is no need for you to search frantically through your mind to check where you have gone wrong. It's much better to ask.

Also remember that it may not be your fault, or anybody else's, when someone is sulky or withdrawn. Remember how stress is activated (*page 13*)? A person may well have become upset because they have just been reminded of a stressful event in their past. This is not your responsibility or your fault. It is therefore also not necessary for you to please them in order to bring them out of it.

Making efforts to be nice to someone is fine, provided they

have told you what their bad mood is about. If they won't tell you but hint that you are the reason for it, don't try and please them as this is often misinterpreted as admitting guilt.

Whether someone complains about everything or sulks silently, I would suggest the following way of dealing with it:

- Give them feedback that they seem to be a bit 'upset' (if they criticise you), 'unhappy' (if they complain) or 'quiet' (if they sulk) and ask if anything is wrong. Under no circumstance should you use the words 'bad mood' – it will only make matters worse because they will feel criticised.

- If they tell you why they are upset, unhappy or quiet, take it from there. If you have done something wrong, apologise. If you don't feel you have done anything wrong, say so. If they have their own reasons for being upset, unhappy or quiet, be supportive if you can.

- If they refuse to tell you what the problem is, relax. There is something you don't know about that makes them unhappy. That is their something, not yours. If you want to, you can try and distract them by suggesting something to do. If this doesn't work, relax. Continue to speak to them normally.

- If they moan about everything, do not agree or disagree with anything they say. Change the topic or go off and do your own thing.

- If they continue to sulk and you cannot distract them, just go and do your own thing. Continue to speak to them in a calm and friendly way when necessary, but do not try to please them. This is their bad mood, not yours.

Dealing with difficult people

Sometimes we need to interact on a daily basis with colleagues, neighbours or relatives who upset us by the way they speak to us or by their mannerisms. Perhaps you are particularly suscep-tible to their negative behaviour because your life is not working out as you want it to and their behaviour acts as a trigger, allowing your original upset to spill out. However, there are also genuine cases of people who, through their behaviour, create general disharmony and unease. How can you deal with them?

Bullies

Bullies will hassle anyone who will let them. If they are confronted, they usually become very apologetic and co-operative, but most people don't dare contradict a bully.

Bullies are insecure people who have been bullied themselves as children, either by their parents, siblings or peers. This may be difficult to believe when you see a bully in action, giving everyone else a hard time. But it is because bullies have themselves been made to feel powerless in the past, that they intimidate others. This restores their sense of power. Whoever proves to be a good victim by showing fear will be bullied again and again. This can be a horrendous ordeal for children because the bullying mostly happens secretly and the victim feels so ashamed of being humiliated that they usually do not tell anyone about it and even deny it when questioned by a concerned adult.

Bullying is not confined to the playground, though. It can take quite a sophisticated shape in adults who, for example, get their own way by making snide remarks if you prove unable to get to grips with the unreasonable amount of work they have given you. Some people may do their bullying in a jolly manner: 'Here, let me cook dinner. You won't know how to do it properly!'

Once someone has established a habit of bullying you, they won't stop until you show some signs that you are no longer prepared to put up with it. Here's how to do it:

- Don't smile at the bully. Many victims try to appease a bully by smiling, but that just marks you out as a victim.
- Maintain eye contact. This denotes that you are taking back power. It can be quite difficult because most victims of bullying start hating the bully after a while and avert their eyes so the bully cannot see the hate there.
- Whatever you say, don't shout. Shouting puts you in a weaker position because you have lost your cool and this is where the bully wants you anyway.

- Ask the bully for a private word. Whether the bully is your boss or your older sister, the issue needs to be addressed before the situation gets out of hand. If you feel very afraid of the bully, you may want to ask a friend or colleague or another family member to come with you to back you up. State clearly that you feel pushed around and that you want this to stop. It doesn't matter if you burst into tears. Say what you have to say anyway.

Backstabbers

These are people with an inferiority complex who say 'yes' when they really want to say 'no'. They are incapable of voicing their true opinion when they disagree with someone, especially if that person is someone in authority. Sweet as pie while in the other person's presence, they turn around completely afterwards and make critical or slanderous comments.

Backstabbers create stress wherever they go because even if their criticism is justified, everyone will grow tired of their gossip and their negative remarks which are never supported by constructive action. It also makes other people wonder what the backstabber might be saying about them behind *their* back ...

To deal with a backstabber:

- State clearly that you are not interested in gossip. Unless you express this in plain language, the backstabber will assume that you approve and agree with them.

- Don't worry that the backstabber will now start criticising you behind your back – they are probably already doing so anyway.

- Point out that any complaints the backstabber has need to be taken up with the person concerned if anything is to change for the better.

- Leave the room if the backstabber does not respond to your request to stop criticising someone. You don't have to listen to them.

- If you yourself are on the receiving end of backstabbing, do not let it ride. Check carefully what has been said about you.

Tell the person who told you about the backstabber's alleged criticism that you will now go and take the matter up with them. If people know you will pursue any gossip, they will often stop passing it around.

- Arrange a meeting with the backstabber and ask for an explanation. Make clear that you prefer to be told directly if something is wrong, rather than to hear it from someone else.

Shirkers

Shirkers are masters of excuse. Whenever work needs doing or a helping hand is required, they suddenly remember a dentist's appointment, develop a headache or claim that they are very busy themselves right now. Shirkers feel (or pretend to feel) that they are hopelessly overworked, when in reality everyone else is doing double the amount of work in the same time.

Shirkers find it very easy to say 'no' to anything that would mean they had to pull their finger out. They behave like spoilt brats, and basically that is what they are. They have often been overindulged as children and are totally oblivious to other people's needs.

If you have to work with a shirker or if someone in your family is not pulling their weight, you are likely to become frustrated after a while because you are the one who does all the running around while the shirker complains about their impossible workload. If the shirker is your boss, you will do all the work while they take all the credit, sometimes without bothering to mention your name in acknowledgement when the project is completed.

How to deal with a shirker:

- Get your facts straight. Take some time to think carefully whether you are justified in resenting the shirker. Are they really not doing enough or is there a genuine reason why they cannot contribute more?

- If you are satisfied that the shirker is not pulling their weight, have a private word with them and find out if there is a reason why they seem unwilling to help. It may be something other than laziness.

- Describe your position in a constructive way, explaining briefly how the shirker's unhelpful ways affect you. If you can do this calmly, it would be to your advantage.

- Negotiate a better deal. Explain clearly what you need from the shirker to resolve the situation. Negotiate until you can agree on a new plan for working together. You may have to compromise, but don't compromise too much. Remember that any improvement is good news, though, and you can always renegotiate later.

Are you an energy vampyr?

What is an energy vampyr? You may have experienced one yourself. A friend rings you up and, without as much as a 'Hello, how are you?', launches into a tirade about what their mother has done now, how their children are so uncaring or how their best friend has, yet again, had a run-in with their boss. This monologue hurtles along at a hundred miles an hour, usually when you have no time to talk or when you are just about to step into the bath. Everything is recounted in the minutest detail, even about people you have never met and are unlikely to ever encounter. Nowhere in this one-sided diatribe is there the slightest interest in how *you* are or what *you* are doing. At the end of this phone call, you feel depleted and utterly depressed. It is as if someone had dumped a big lorry load of rubbish in your emotional front room.

The same thing can of course also happen with a neighbour or a work colleague who innocently pops through your front door or into your office and starts talking nineteen to the dozen.

The way to spot an energy vampyr is simple. Check the following points:

- They go on about the same thing time and time again. It is like listening to the latest instalment of a soap opera.

- They gossip a lot.

- They talk continuously.

- They never take a blind bit of notice of any advice you give them but launch into their tale of woe as if you hadn't spoken.

- They constantly demand your attention.

- They turn every little thing in their life into a mini-drama.

- They get really angry if you cancel a date with them and insist you turn up anyway, no matter what your reason for cancelling.

Energy vampyrs are not easy to get rid of. They never seem to come up for air and it can be extremely difficult to stop them in their tracks without feeling that you are being rude. They tend to ambush you in the evening or even late at night when they can be sure you will be in. They reckon just because they are up, you have to be up too, and anyway, they are having such a horrific time that as a friend, you owe it to them to listen to their problems.

Here are some tips on how to deal with energy vampyrs:

- Make it a rule that you never answer the phone after a particular time at night. Let the answering machine pick up calls. You can listen in as people leave messages and always pick up the phone yourself if it is a real emergency.

- Do not avoid energy vampyrs. It doesn't work. You need to face them. Talk over them if you must, but say firmly that you have no time to talk at the moment, and could they please ring back or call round 'some other time'.

- If you feel you are being rude, think of how rude it is of the energy vampyr to suck you dry without even enquiring how you are!

- Don't be afraid of losing the vampyr's friendship. They are not good for you anyway. If they never speak to you again, this would be the best thing that could happen to you. As they gossip about everyone, they are certain to gossip about you too. You are really better off without them.

The problem with having an energy vampyr on your back is that it can turn you into one as well! Because you are annoyed by those midnight calls and endless laments, you may be tempted to dump your annoyance onto another friend. Beware! Look through the checklist above and make sure you don't do the same thing to others.

If you have a complaint about someone, log your complaint with the person concerned. It's no good telling everyone else that a friend is getting on your nerves. Tell your friend – only then can things change.

Dealing constructively with your emotions will go a long way towards resolving stress issues. As you *feel* calmer, your intellect will work more efficiently and you will resolve difficult situations more easily. Make sure, though, that you also give your body due attention. During and after stressful periods, you can become run down and depleted of nutrients and water. The next chapter will explain how you can look after your body during 'rollercoaster' times.

CHAPTER FIVE

Supporting the body

When your mind and emotions have been in overdrive for a while, your body will have to work harder to keep a physical equilibrium. The more stressed you feel, the greater the demands on your glands and organs to adapt and rebalance. Short spurts of stress are not so much of a problem as long stretches of being in overdrive. This is one reason why it is so important to take breaks and allow yourself time to rest, *especially* when you feel you have no time to relax. When you rest, you give not only your mind the chance to calm down, but also your body the opportunity to recover strength.

There are two ways in which you can help your body cope better when you are under stress. One is to take time to release physical tension mechanically by doing some gentle exercise and taking enough rest; the other is to become choosier about what you put into your body.

A general rule for nutritional support is to drink enough water and avoid processed foods as much as possible. If you are not sure whether something is processed or not, ask yourself: does this grow in this form on a tree, a shrub or in the earth? This leaves you with fruit and vegetables as natural and everything else as processed. Ask yourself further: does this look like part or all of an animal? This leaves you with a leg of lamb or a fish as natural, and a burger as processed.

This section of the book is particularly relevant to you if you notice any of the following symptoms:

- You feel tired or exhausted most of the time.

- You have become very sensitive to noise and/or light.

- Your eating habits have changed – you overeat or don't eat at all.

- You are short of breath without having exerted yourself.

- Resting does not improve your energy levels.

- You catch any illness that is going.

- An existing illness becomes worse.

Physical quick fixes

- Dwell on a pleasant memory and feel how your body starts relaxing.

- Do something playful for at least 15 minutes.

- Eat more slowly. Walk more slowly.

- Take a nap if you can. Taking a nap when you are tired is a sign of intelligence, not laziness.

- Laugh about something. If you can't find anything funny, laugh about yourself.

- Every time you think you need a break but don't have time for one, stop what you are doing for five minutes.

- Walk barefoot across grass. This gets you in contact with different physical sensations and stimulates your energies in a positive way.

- Stroke gently across your head, from front to back. Do this several times.

- Hum a tune. Humming causes relaxing vibrations in the throat.

- Avoid sweets and monosodium glutamate (MSG) in your diet. They make you edgy.

- After a stressful day, dim bright lights or light candles. Soft light is more relaxing and will help you unwind.

- Take a very warm footbath which contains a tablespoon of salt last thing at night. This can reduce your need to go to the toilet at night.

- Eat slowly and eat regularly. This puts less pressure on your digestion. Don't eat when you are stressed; wait until you are a bit calmer.

- If you work in artificial light, make sure you get some daylight into your eyes by going outside for a little walk during your break.

- Drink at least eight glasses of water during the day, more if you are stressed (*see also page* 127).

Practical exercises and tips

Wake-up Call exercises

If you have been sitting for a long time, either at work, in a meeting, driving the car or operating machinery or a computer, your body 'freezes' in a particular position and needs to be released so that circulation and breathing can work properly again. 'Freezing' can cause physical stress in the long term, so it is a good idea to counteract it on a regular basis to prevent stress from building up in the first place.

Here is a little routine that can help your body wake up again. All three exercises together take only a little more than a minute to do.

Wake-up 1

- Rub your hands together to create energy between them.

- Bend forward and loosely pummel the back of your thighs with your fists. Walk your fists several times up and down the back of your thighs.

Wake-up 2

- Interlock your fingers and turn them outwards.

- Now stretch your hands over your head, very slowly and very gently. Follow your hands with your eyes and keep your eyes looking upwards, head tilted back. Can you straighten your arms?

- Stay in this position to a count of 30.

Wake-up 3

- Rub your hands together to create energy between them.

- Place your hands on your back over your kidneys. Lean forward a little.

- Imagine breathing energy into your kidneys until your kidneys are full and your hands are empty.

Belly breathing

We have already looked at a simple breathing exercise in the mental exercises section (*see page 47*), but I would now like to show you an even more powerful exercise which is beneficial for the entire body. Doing this exercise will not only help you stay healthier and more relaxed, but it will also increase your awareness of the capacity of your lungs.

When you are stressed, your breathing is fast and takes place mainly in the upper part of the lungs, reducing your intake of oxygen. When not enough oxygen gets into the bloodstream, the body becomes an ideal breeding ground for illness, including cancer! So take a little break every once in a while during your hectic day and do the following:

- Put your hands on your lower ribcage, left hand on left side, right hand on right.

- Breathe out completely, pushing the air out all the way.

- Close your eyes and breathe in slowly through the nose. Imagine that your lungs are balloons that are now beginning to fill up from the bottom. Concentrate on expanding these inner balloons as far as possible.

- When your lungs feel full, stop. Open your mouth and take one last breath in, topping up the air supply in your lungs.

- Hold your breath for a moment and then exhale completely through the mouth, contracting the muscle of your stomach to press out every last bit out air.

- Repeat five times.

If you have been stressed for a while, you may well find that you feel a bit dizzy or faint doing this exercise. This is an indication that you have not been breathing properly for quite a long time and your body and brain have not had an appropriate supply of oxygen. This exercise provides you with a large amount of oxygen, which feels normal when you are generally breathing properly. But if you tend to give your brain little oxygen due to physical and emotional tension, your brain is 'shocked' by the sudden influx of oxygen, and this is what can make you feel dizzy or faint. Don't worry about it – it just shows that you need to do this exercise very regularly. To start with, simply reduce the amount of oxygen you take in. Don't fill your lungs all the way, but make sure you still exhale all the way out. After doing a reduced version of the exercise, you will soon be able to fill your lungs to the brim and feel invigorated rather than dizzy.

Acupressure and reflexology

Acupressure and reflexology work on the principle that illness, stress or injury can leave the body in a state of imbalance so that vital energy pathways are blocked and healing processes cannot progress. This imbalance can be detected by the build-up of tiny crystalline deposits in an area of the body that relates to the organ or body part that is affected. By working and massaging the reflex points, the blockages are released and the free flow of energy restored so that the body can get well again.

In general, reflexologists prefer to work on the feet rather than on the hands because they are more sensitive and the reflex areas are larger, but I want you to be able to relieve stress quickly and on the spot and I'm sure you'll agree that your hands are more easily accessible than your feet, especially if you are sitting in an important board meeting!

The following reflexology self-massage exercises will help you when you feel generally stressed, when you are suffering from a tension headache or if you are exhausted.

For general stress

- Find the centre of the inside of your palm by placing the thumb of the other hand (Figure 3; point C). This area of your palm corresponds to your solar plexus.

- Massage this point by rotating your thumb for two to three minutes.

- Repeat on the other hand.

For headaches

- Feel around the top section of your thumb until you find a sensitive area.

- Massage this point firmly with your other thumb for about a minute.

- Repeat on the other hand.

For exhaustion

When you feel pumped out and exhausted, help your body recover its strength by massaging the areas on your hands which relate to your kidneys, spleen, pancreas, liver and stomach. Work your way around your hands as follows:

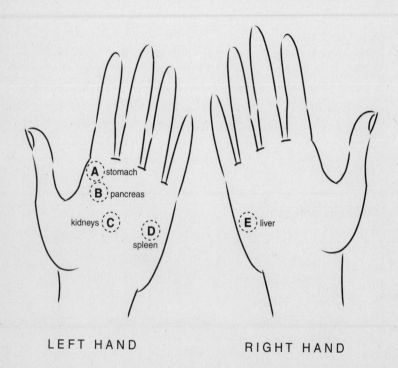

Figure 3. Acupressure and reflexology

Left hand

Start off by massaging your left hand. (Although if you are left-handed and want to start on your right hand first, that's OK as well.)

- Massage the inside of your left palm in area A for the stomach, using your *right* thumb.

- Now move down a little lower and massage area B for the pancreas, moving towards the centre of your left palm as you dig into the hand with your right thumb.

- Now move further to the very centre of your left palm and knead the middle of your palm to activate area C which relates to your kidneys.

- Continue by moving further over to the side of the left hand and massage area D, which is associated with the spleen.

Right hand

Now change over to massage your right hand.

Go to area E, which is associated with the liver, and massage around this area with the thumb of your left hand.

Yoga

The following exercise will help you to relax physically and to counteract stress by helping to limber up the spine. By carrying out the movements gently, slowly and as smoothly as possible, you create a healing stretch through the entire length of the back, which encourages the circulation of blood from the base of the spine to your head. At the same time, it has a calming influence on the mind.

From child pose to cat pose

Warm up by doing the wake-up exercises first (*see page 110*) and then go on as follows:

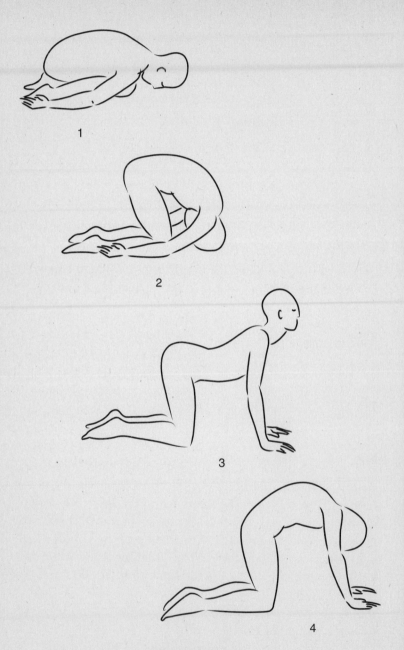

Figure 4. Yoga

1. The Child Pose
- Sit back on your lower legs, legs slightly apart.

- Put your forehead on the floor and rest your arms on the floor, pointing backwards. Breathe normally.

- Stay in this pose for 10 breath cycles.

2. The Raised Child Pose
- Now lift your hips towards the ceiling and roll your head forward so that you lightly rest on the crown of your head.

- Keep your arms relaxed by your side and feel the gentle stretch in the back of your neck. *Keep on breathing normally.*

- Hold this pose for 10 breath cycles.

3. The Cat Pose
- Come onto all fours, hands directly beneath your shoulders.

- Start with your head in line with your spine, looking at the floor.

- *Very slowly*, begin to raise your head up. You can feel your spine stretching out and curving gently in the direction of the floor while your head and tailbone are moving up. *Keep on breathing normally.*

- Only do this to a level where you still feel comfortable and relaxed.

- Breathe 10 times in and out while gently holding the posture.

4. Reverse Cat Pose
- As you exhale, squeeze your chin to your chest, arch your spine and tuck in your tailbone. *Keep on breathing normally.*

- Hold this pose for another 10 breath cycles.

- Now release again and return to the Child Pose.

- Rest for 10 breath cycles and get up *slowly*.

Snacks that help you sleep

Stress is made worse if you can't sleep. As the body uses night-time to repair itself and regenerate energy, you will be much more nervy the next morning if you have not slept soundly.

Many foods contain compounds that have a relaxing effect on the brain. This means that if you can eat the right things before you go to bed, you are more likely to have a good night's sleep. Scientists have found that natural sedatives in foods work by stimulating the brain to produce calming chemicals which promote a feeling of drowsiness. Try one of these healthy snacks about 40 minutes before you settle down under your duvet.

Onion and tomato salad

Slice 3 tomatoes and 1 small red onion. Sprinkle with fresh, chopped basil and drizzle with olive oil.
Why it helps: Onions were used by the ancient Egyptians to aid relaxation and sleep. They contain quercetin, which is a mild sedative. Red and yellow varieties are the richest source of this compound.

Honey with oatcakes

Spread 2 oatcakes with a generous helping of pure honey.
Why it helps: Thanks to its high sugar content, honey boosts levels of the feelgood chemical serotonin, inducing feelings of tranquillity and drowsiness. A study found that honey can be as effective as a sleeping pill but without the side-effect of grogginess in the morning.

Celery and houmous

Slice 2 sticks of celery and 1 carrot into long pieces and dip them into houmous.

Why it helps: Celery has a calming effect because it contains a substance called 3-n-butylphthalide, which acts as a gentle sedative.

Physical self-sabotage

Smoking

There is only one sensible thing to do about smoking – *quit!* I know you have heard all the stories about how bad it is for you, but did you know that two to three drops of pure nicotine alcohol on the tongue will kill an adult in minutes?

The long-term effects of smoking are by now well known. As a smoker, you have an increased risk of:

heart attacks

strokes

stomach ulcers

impaired healing of wounds

poor digestion

bad breath(!)

If you are pregnant and continue to smoke, you also risk mental and physical defects of the foetus, premature birth, miscarriage and stillbirth.

You also lose your sense of smell and taste to a certain extent because the lining of your nose and the tastebuds on your tongue get coated in a layer of about 4,000 chemicals, among them nicotine, a highly toxic nerve poison. In the past, vets used neat nicotine to put down animals!

The good news is that only 20 minutes after you have stopped smoking that last cigarette, your body begins an ongoing series of beneficial changes:

20 minutes later

blood pressure drops to normal

pulse rate drops to normal

temperature of hands and feet increases to normal

8 hours later

carbon-monoxide level in the blood drops to normal

oxygen level in the blood increases to normal

24 hours later

the chance of a heart attack decreases

2 weeks to 3 months later

circulation improves

lung function increases by up to 30 per cent

1–9 months later

coughing, sinus congestion, fatigue, shortness of breath decrease

cilia regrow in the lungs, increasing the ability to handle mucus, clean the lungs and reduce infection

1 year later

the risk of coronary heart disease decreases

If you find it hard to give up smoking, get help. Hypnotherapy is an excellent way of getting off the weed, as are laser therapy and acupuncture, to name just a few.

The following tips may help you give up cigarettes:

- Realise that you are an adult who is a slave to little rolled-up dried leaves. Very uncool!

- Spend time remembering the very first cigarette you ever had and how disgusting it tasted.

- Be aware of the stale tobacco smoke on people around you and how it clings to hair, clothes and the breath of every smoker. Embarrassing to think that you emit this odour yourself …

- From now on, hold your cigarette in the other hand.

- Switch to a brand you don't like.

- Slowly limit the times and places where you can have a cigarette. Stop smoking in the car, stop smoking in the mornings, etc.

- Postpone having the next cigarette.

- Keep your lighter in the garden shed and the cigarettes at the back of a kitchen cupboard. Make it harder to just reach for them.

- Get up once you have eaten to avoid the post-dinner cigarette/s.

And finally, if all else fails:

- Imagine what it will feel like when you sit in your doctor's waiting-room, waiting for the biopsy results. Imagine the doctor coming out and giving you the worst news imaginable. Imagine knowing that it could all have been avoided!

- Imagine you had died of a smoking-related disease. (An average of 12 people die *every hour* in Britain as a result of a smoking-related disease.) Imagine your children being told by your partner's new boyfriend or girlfriend what to do ...

- Imagine your partner in bed with someone else – which they will be once they have got over you having smoked yourself to death ...

- If you can't give up by yourself, get outside help. (*See Useful Addresses, page 172.*)

Neglecting your life rhythm

Think for a moment what it is like when you feel unhurried, untroubled and reasonably content with your life. What is a normal weekday like? You will probably get up at a certain time, have a shower, eat something, get yourself ready for work and then set off or, if you are working from home, get into your office or workshop. During the course of the day, you will have a few longer or shorter breaks to eat and drink something, then pack it in at a certain time to return home. Then you relax a little and start thinking about dinner, eat, potter around and then go to bed and sleep. OK, end of fairy tale. This is how it should be when you are feeling calm and collected – your days and nights have a rhythm and a flow which carry you comfortably along. I call this the life rhythm.

A working day needs to be punctuated by relaxing breaks, by times when you feed your body and other times when you do something that has nothing to do with work. Weekends are different, but they, too, need to have their own rhythm. The weekend should allow for longer sleep, a more leisurely pace, with lots of rest or activities that are not work-related. These weekday and weekend life rhythms will of course vary from person to person, but they need to have some basic component in order for you to stay healthy: reasonable predictability, regular food intake, regular (non-alcoholic) fluid intake, breaks for relaxation and switching off and sufficient sleep. Although the body is enormously adaptable, you will become unwell if you do not provide these vital components on a reasonably regular basis.

When we are stressed, our life rhythm can get out of synch because we start overriding one or several of the vital components of our day. We have too much to do or too much to worry about, so we skip breakfast, skip the morning break, skip lunch, forget to take in liquids, work longer hours, take work home, either in our briefcase or our head, wolf down a microwave meal or whatever is in the fridge and then are unable to sleep. If work piles up even more, we may even override the entire weekend rhythm and skip the relaxation time, the sleeping in, and so on. But no one can get away with disrupting their life rhythm like that forever.

Overriding your life rhythm will simply make stress worse. And there is no need to do it. While I recognise that stress can prevent you from sleeping, everything else is under your direct control. It is your decision to skip meals and not take breaks.

There are several reasons why it is important to maintain a daily rhythm. For one thing, it gives you a structure to hang on to when everything else might be in the air. We need a daily framework that, on the whole, stays the same – especially today, when we have to be so much more adaptable than even only 50 years ago. So many facets in our lives keep changing. We move with our work much more than in the past, we travel more extensively, technology is changing incredibly quickly, our family is spread all over the country or even all over the world. There are very few constants left in our lives that, in the past, gave our days a structure. On top of that, our increased demands for a good standard of living dictate that two people need to work rather than just one, so there are often two stressed people per household rather than just one. The life rhythm can work like a thread that holds it all together, a constant that reminds you that there is such a thing as normality.

Another reason why a life rhythm is important is that it ensures that you look after your body. Your body needs to be fed and watered regularly, especially when you are stressed. It's your body that supports your mental performance during the day. We wouldn't dream of expecting a car to run without petrol, but we seem to take for granted that our bodies can run on empty. Cars will simply stop working without oil or petrol, but our bodies will substitute the lack of energy coming in via food and rest by mobilising its reserves. This is fine for a week or two, but if the stress goes on, you will deplete your energy reserves unless you eat and rest again.

To check what elements constitute your personal life rhythm, establish the following:

- How many sit-down meals do you have during a normal working day when you are *not* stressed?

- How many breaks do you take during a normal working day when you are *not* stressed?

- How many sit-down meals do you have during a relaxed weekend?

- Can you get a lie-in at the weekend if you want to?

- Can you do what you want to do on a weekend day?

I'm assuming here that you work from Monday to Friday and have Saturday and Sunday off. If you work shifts or if you have weekdays off rather than weekends, still answer the questions. It doesn't matter if you don't have a conventional life rhythm – the main thing is that there is some sort of rhythm to your days that contains rest, food, fluid intake and sleep. If you travel a lot, your working day may well be much more change-able than that of a nine-to-five worker. You will still need some sort of life rhythm, though!

Take the time to detect what constitutes your pattern and make it a priority to stick to it as closely as possible when things get hectic. If it is not possible to have lunch at lunchtime, make sure you have it later and *don't* just rush on with the next chore. Your brain needs breaks and so does your body. If you are not getting the breaks, something is wrong. Either you are overstretching yourself or someone else is. And no one will thank you for ruining your health in order to do your job. If you make yourself too ill to work, they will simply replace you with someone else.

Once you have run down your body, it takes a long time to get better. It makes more sense to look after your health on a day-to-day basis than when it is too late. Don't ruin your health in order to please others or to make money, because you will only end up spending all that money to get your health back!

Sugar – destruction from within

When you are stressed and need a quick boost, it's tempting to reach for a sugary snack. But sugar is not good for you. This has been drummed into us for decades now, but the only thing that most people are aware of is the detrimental effect sugar has on your teeth. But the detrimental effects of sugar are much more far-reaching than rotting teeth.

White crystalline sugar is refined from cane or beet by strip-ping away all the fibres, proteins and other healthy elements. The remaining substance is then bleached with charcoal, leaving only a single industrially processed chemical. This chemical is then added to all sorts of other processed foods, so that even if you don't take sugar in your tea or coffee, you are still being fed it in other ways.

A little sugar is no problem, but if you consume lots of foods that contain sugar, you begin to do serious damage to your health. The body is not designed to deal with lots of sugar. We derive energy from eating carbohydrates, fat and protein. Starchy carbohydrates are slowly converted into sugars in the body and this in turn gives us energy. This conversion process takes two to three hours – enough time for our metabolism to deal with the sugars.

It is quite a different matter with refined sugar. As it has much smaller molecules, the body converts them quickly so that they arrive in the bloodstream in less than an hour. But our metabolism cannot cope with this flooding of sugar and 'panics'. The pancreas starts producing masses of insulin. This hormone makes the muscles and the liver hang on to the sugar and either store it or convert it into body fat. Only a little sugar is stored – most of it is converted into fat.

If you eat sugar regularly, the pancreas goes into overdrive and produces masses of insulin. This means that too much sugar is locked into the liver and muscles and too little is available as energy in the blood. In other words, if you eat sugar regularly in larger quantities, you develop hypoglycaemia. This means chronic tiredness, irritability, dizziness and sometimes even fainting spells. Too much sugar also leads to undernourishment due to the leeching of vitamins and minerals from the body.

If sugar is so bad for you, you may think that you are better off using artificial sweeteners in your teas, coffees and soft drinks labelled 'diet' or 'sugar free'. But if sugar is bad, artificial sweeteners are even worse, and there is extensive research to prove it.

The most widely used sweetener is aspartame, which is added to drinks and food as a sugar substitute. Aspartame is also in other sweeteners, so check the label of any 'diet' foods or drinks you buy. The problem is that aspartame is actually an extremely toxic chemical. Although it is marketed as a diet product, it causes weight *gain* because it makes you crave carbohydrates. But that is the least of your problems. Aspartame alters the brain's chemistry by changing the dopamine level in the brain, which can cause seizures.

The reason why aspartame is extremely poisonous is that it contains wood alcohol. When the temperature of aspartame exceeds 86°F, the wood alcohol converts to formaldehyde – this is what is used as embalming fluid for corpses! Formaldehyde is grouped in the same class of poisons as cyanide and arsenic. Just like these poisons, aspartame attacks and destroys the nervous system, but unlike them it does so slowly.

Symptoms that can be caused by aspartame poisoning are spasms, shooting pains, numbness in your legs, cramps, vertigo, dizziness, headaches, tinnitus, joint pain, depression, anxiety attacks, slurred speech, blurred vision or memory loss. All this could be diagnosed as stress symptoms or even fibromyalgia, when it is really aspartame poisoning.

Aspartame poisoning is also often diagnosed as multiple sclerosis. The methanol toxicity mimics MS, but once you come off the aspartame, most of the symptoms disappear. There are cases where vision and hearing have returned after giving up artificial sweeteners.

Try and avoid sugar as far as possible and cut down drastically on your use of it in tea and coffee. Make it a habit to check ingredients labels for sugar, glucose, fructose or dextrose. Remember that ingredients are listed in order of greatest quantity, so if anything has sugar as the first ingredient, put it straight back onto the shelf! Be particularly careful if a product says 'sugar free' – it usually means that sugar has been substituted by an artificial sweetener. Don't touch anything with a bargepole that says 'diet' on it, unless this refers to reduced fat.

If you can't live without sweet things, go for jams that are sweetened with fruit juice. Every spoonful of sugar that does *not* end up in your body is good news!

Stress and dehydration

Most of us have heard about those famous eight glasses of water we are supposed to drink every day, but few people really know *why* this is important. I would like to explain the reasons here because drinking water is one of the simplest ways of helping yourself to de-stress.

The human body consists of 25 per cent solid matter and 75 per cent water. Brain tissue is said to be composed of 85 per cent water. Every living cell requires water. In order to function properly, the body needs to be replenished with water throughout the day. The body functions because electrical impulses are sent through the network of nerve fibres which in turn trigger the activity of many organs and glands. In order to relay information efficiently, these electrical impulses need water as a conductor. Water also helps all the organs in the body work more efficiently by lubricating the digestive tract and detoxifying the body.

If you are dehydrated, all sorts of illnesses can follow. The kidneys start producing highly concentrated urine, which can cause infections such as cystitis. It can also trigger kidney stones, which form when the calcium in urine collects into small lumps. Drinking plenty of water keeps calcium dissolved, making stones less likely. Dehydration also leads to constipation, as the soluble fibre in your diet cannot soak up water which would help it be propelled more easily through the bowel.

When you don't drink enough, the body goes into an emergency state – it hangs on to any water it has. This is when we speak of 'water retention'. One reason for this can obviously be the overuse of salt, but if this is not the case, the only way to reverse water retention is to drink plenty of water. This 'reassures' the body that it is OK to let go of the stored water.

Stress uses up a lot of water in the body simply because higher demands are made on our nerves. When we are under pressure, the body is in a state of high alert, so that the nerves are working overtime, using up our water resources much faster than they would normally do. Unless you replenish this lost fluid, the brain cannot function properly. This is the reason why we get a headache and feel muddle-headed or confused when we are stressed. You may have seen how someone in shock is given a glass of water. This is excellent first aid for someone who has just experienced trauma, as a shock will deplete the body of most of its water in one fell swoop.

Water should be taken regularly throughout the day, whether you feel thirsty or not. When you are stressed, you need to drink even more than the usual eight glasses.

The following environmental and nutritional factors will also require you to drink more than just eight glasses of water because they dehydrate the body:

eating foods that contain chemicals and additives

eating processed foods

living or working in a centrally heated environment

living or working in an air-conditioned environment

hot weather

exercising

drinking tea, coffee and/or alcohol

Still water is much better than sparkling water, but if you vastly prefer sparkling, then have it. It is better to have fizzy water (but without sugar or flavours) than no water at all. The reason why I recommend still water is that it is easier on the stomach and bowels, and when you are stressed it is particularly important to supply your body with liquid that is easy to digest.

Water cannot be replaced by juices or soft drinks. Even though they contain water, they also contain dehydrating agents. If you find it difficult or unpleasant to drink water, use a straw. That way the water does not touch the inside of your mouth and goes straight down your throat, which can make it much easier to get down.

When you start drinking water regularly, it makes sense to ensure that the quality of your water is as good as possible. Water acts as a solvent in the body, and the purer it is – free from minerals, softeners and pollutants – the more toxins can be carried out of the cells. Filter your tap water or, even better, have a device installed that gives you live water (*see Useful Addresses, p. 170*). This is water that has been magnetically treated to enhance its quality.

Dr Batmanghelidj, an authority on water, recommends in his book *Your Body's Many Cries for Water* that you also add some salt to your diet. He points out that salt is an essential ingredient for the body, ranking in importance just behind oxygen and water. Twenty-seven per cent of the salt content of the body is stored in the bones as crystals, and salt crystals are part of what makes bone hard. This means that if salt has to be taken out of the bones in order to maintain vital normal salt levels in the blood, it will weaken them. Salt deficiency could therefore be involved in oesteoporosis. Dr Batmanghelidj recommends approximately $\frac{1}{4}$ teaspoon of salt per day if you drink two litres of water in order to ensure a balanced intake. However, before you rush over to your saltcellar, please check how much salt you are taking in when you eat during the day. Many processed foods contain salt, and you may already be using that quarter teaspoonful in what you are putting on your meals!

Food for thought

How healthy are dairy products?

Milk and milk products are said to be good for you. It is claimed that cow's milk is full of calcium, which will give you healthy bones, and that it contains vitamins B12 and riboflavin, which give you energy and boost your immune system.

The fact is that 7 out of 10 people suffer from an allergy to cow's milk. When I test clients at my kinesiology practice, most of them have a problem with milk, yoghurt and cheese.

The fact is that human beings lose their metabolic ability to process the lactose in their own mother's milk by the age of four. Cow's milk is fine for calves, who are herbivores with four stomachs and a huge bone mass, but not for human beings, who do not possess this enormous digestive apparatus.

If you experience any of the following signs after you have consumed milk or milk products, you may suffer from a milk allergy or intolerance:

itchy red rash

hives

eczema

runny nose

wheezy breathing

bloating

vomiting

diarrhoea

cramps

nasal stuffiness

clogged-up ears

recurrent ear infections

recurrent colds

recurrent bronchitis

Cow's milk allergy is one of the most common food allergies in children. Even if a baby is not being fed cow's milk, small amounts of milk protein can pass through the breastmilk from the mother to her baby and may cause allergic signs and symptoms. If so, the mother needs to exclude all dairy products from her diet and take a calcium supplement.

There is now evidence that frequent milk and dairy consumption more than doubles the risk of prostate cancer. The problem lies in milk's effect on the insulin growth factor IGF-1. IGF-1 occurs naturally in human and in cow's milk, and once genetic protection has been breached, it accelerates malignant cell growth. Milk raises IGF-1 levels and at the same time, the excessive calcium suppresses vitamin D activity, which in turn reinforces malignant cell growth.

A lot is made of our need to take in calcium to maintain strong bones. However, not a lot of the calcium in cow's milk actually remains in the body. There are several substances in milk, particularly the protein, which contribute to calcium *loss*. A third of the calcium that you initially absorb when drinking milk is excreted again by the body via urine. In cheese, more than two-thirds of the calcium gained is wasted again. If you are *allergic* to milk products (which the majority of people are), you won't absorb anything at all, because your body expels the whole lot at lightning speed to rid itself of the allergen.

Dairy products alone won't save your bones, either. *The American Journal of Clinical Nutrition* concluded recently that it is excess calcium *loss* that causes age-related bone loss rather than inadequate calcium *intake*.

In order to keep bones healthy and strong we need to cut down on animal protein, as this robs us of calcium, and increase our potassium levels by eating a diet rich in fruit and vegetables. Apart from that, we also need to ensure that we get vitamin D, which means a good 15 minutes outside in the sunshine or, in winter, taking vitamin D supplements. Eating your greens will also help calcium absorption. The only exception is spinach, which you should only eat in very moderate quantities as it contains considerable amounts of uric acid, which can lead to gout and arthritis.

Another saviour of bone strength is vitamin K, which is present in dark leafy vegetables. Just 100 grams of leafy vegetables per day provides enough vitamin K to halve the risk of fractures. Although a pint of milk contains twice as much calcium as 200 grams of spring greens, they are nevertheless better at helping you preserve calcium in your bones because they are lower in protein and higher in potassium. You will also need to 'use' your bones in order to keep them strong. Simple walking will do the trick – 15 to 20 minutes a day is enough.

When you are intolerant or allergic to milk, it forms mucus in the body which clogs up your bowels. This ultimately means that vital elimination processes are severely hampered, with a residue of waste materials remaining in the system. This compromises your health because the body is unable to run smoothly when there is mucus cluttering up the elimination channels.

If you are allergic to cow's milk, you may also be allergic to goat's or sheep's milk, so this is not necessarily an alternative. From my experience, anything called 'milk', even when it is plant derived like soya milk, can be a problem. Your best bet is to see a kinesiologist and have a test to see which sorts of milk agree with you. Or better still, learn to muscle-test yourself so you can check foods to see whether you are allergic to something or not (*see Useful Addresses, page 168*).

Also, don't forget that anything you eat as part of a staple diet can become an allergen, so make sure you vary what you eat. For breakfast, have cereals with, say, rice milk one morning, some rye bread the next, some fruit the day after, and so on. That way you ensure that your body does not get overloaded with one particular food.

If you can drink cow's milk, and want to, use the low-fat variety, as the saturated fats of full-fat milk put you at a greater risk of a heart attack.

And then there is also the animal welfare aspect. Did you know that the modern high-yield dairy cow is no better off than a battery hen? Milk-producing cows today are genetically engineered to be permanently hungry and graze all day long so they can produce 100 pints of milk a day – twice as much as normal cows would produce! The cows get ill very easily and by the time they are three years old are usually only fit for culling. It's time we started taking the same action we did with battery hens. If we need to drink milk, let's at least drink milk from cows that have a decent life!

Why we need supplements

Several newspapers have been printing reports recently that vitamin pills have 'no health benefits and are a waste of money'. The research these comments referred to was run by the Medical Research Council (MRC) and the British Heart Foundation (BHF) and published in the *Lancet*. Over a five-year period the so-called Heart Protection Study was carried out as a randomised placebo-controlled trial on over 20,000 individuals and concluded that the antioxidant vitamins given to the test group did not improve the subjects' health. What the newspapers did *not* state was that the subjects selected included those diagnosed as having coronary heart disease or strong risk factors for heart disease, such as diabetes. Also not mentioned was the fact that those selected were aged between 40 and 80 years of age, with 28 per cent of them over 70 years. But the most important point the papers missed out on was the fact that, at the start of the five-year study, all the subjects were already clinically diagnosed to be at high risk of death during that period.

In making the huge and illogical jump to conclude from this data that antioxidant nutrients cannot help prevent heart disease and other serious conditions, the media ignored thousands of existing studies that have proved just the opposite. Substantial research evidence shows that consumption of high-dose antioxidant vitamins over more than 10 years helps to reduce the risk of developing heart disease, but should not be used for the treatment of risk factors and diseases that are already established.

Ironically, three weeks before the *Lancet* article was published, two major scientific reviews of the role of vitamins in chronic disease were published in the *Journal of the American Medical Association*. The studies reviewed key nutritional studies from 1966 to 2001 and concluded that vitamins play a key role in the prevention of many diseases. These studies were completely ignored by the media.

The reason why it is necessary to supplement our diet with vitamins, minerals and herbs is not only that they *do* help keep us healthy or restore our health, but also that the food we are eating comes out of depleted and unhealthy soil. For the last 50 years or so, we have been using chemical fertilisers, synthetic herbicides and pesticides and have pumped our cattle full of drugs and vaccines. Before food reaches our tables, it is often refined to death so that there is not a lot left in it that can fulfil our nutritional needs. Even if you eat fruit and vegetables, you end up with produce that was grown in soil that is severely deficient in important nutrients and trace elements.

Countless researchers have focused on vitamins and trace minerals over the past 50 years as being the 'missing link' in the human nutrition puzzle. It has been discovered that chromium, for instance, is a vital trace nutrient, while fluorine, also a trace element, will adversely affect the nervous system as it is stored in the body and builds up over time.

Research in Canada suggests that a number of central nervous system disorders appear to be connected with a lack of vital nutrients. Among these disorders are clinical depression, attention deficit disorder, fibromyalgia, chronic fatigue, schizophrenia, anxiety and Tourette's syndrome. University of Calgary and Utah researchers discovered a common nutritional deficiency in all these illnesses. Treatment with essential vitamins and minerals resulted in a vastly improved mental state, with patients able to function normally again. The advantages of supplements over pharmaceuticals is considerable – not only are they a lot cheaper, but they also don't have any detrimental side-effects, as opposed to chemical drugs.

While not all cases of depression or anxiety may be related to the quality of the food we are eating, it is nevertheless worth thinking about whether we really do get everything we need from our food and whether supplements would be of benefit.

My personal experience with supplements has been excellent so far. Not only do I see great improvements in clients, but I have also been using herbs and minerals over the last few years to combat hot flushes, tiredness and irritability brought on by the menopause. Whereas I started off with hot flushes every half hour, day and night, I was able to get rid of them totally within a single week of taking supplements. This meant I could sleep well again, had more energy and was in a better mood throughout the day.

Mercury and stress

'Mad as a hatter' – this term was coined when British workers in the hat trade used mercury (also known as quicksilver) to make hats. They often experienced mental deterioration and were consequently locked in insane asylums.

Mercury is a powerful biological poison and extremely toxic – more toxic than lead, cadmium and arsenic. It is well known for attacking the central nervous system and causing neuro-toxicity. It easily crosses the blood-brain barrier and deposits into the central nervous system.

Any silver amalgam fillings you have in your mouth are composed of at least 50 per cent mercury. Mercury vapour is released from these fillings, particularly after chewing, grind-ing your teeth, hot and/or acidic food and tooth brushing.

Scrap dental amalgam was declared a hazardous waste in 1988 by the Environmental Protection Agency. Outside your mouth it has to be stored in unbreakable, tightly sealed containers away from heat. It also has to be left untouched and stored under liquid glycerine or photographic fixer solution. So *outside* your mouth it is declared toxic, but when it is placed in the teeth it is labelled 'non-toxic'. It doesn't make a lot of sense, does it …

Amalgam fillings have been tested for their strength but never for their safety. At the University of North Texas, however, tests found that 90 per cent of dentists have neuropsychological dysfunction. Female dentists and dental personnel have higher rates of spontaneous abortion than females in other professions. This is because elemental mercury crosses into the placenta as minute traces of it are released into the body through chewing, teeth brushing or just handling it in the course of work. There is a direct correlation between mercury levels, reproductive failures and menstrual cycle disorders.

Mercury in the body results in an inactivation of proteins such as enzymes, hormones or cell receptors, and their destruc-tion wreaks havoc on the body's energy-producing system. Mercury also destroys the mucous membrane of the gastro-intestinal tract, which is one of our most powerful immune defences. It is especially destructive towards the kidneys, liver and brain. Autopsy studies have shown that the more dental amalgam fillings a person has, the higher the mercury levels in the brain and kidneys.

Apart from dental fillings, other sources of mercury are fungicides and pesticides, cosmetics, seafood (especially tuna), medicines, laxatives, the inks used in some printing and tattoos, some types of paint, some refined grains and seeds, chlorine bleaches, contact lens solutions, felt, fabric softener, floor waxes and polishes, film, broken thermometers and barometers, antiseptic creams and lotions, and nasal sprays.

Signs and symptoms of mercury poisoning are:

fever

chills

fatigue and chronic fatigue

headache

insomnia

loss of sex drive

depression

numbness and tingling in the hands

irritability

asthma

learning difficulties

irregular heartbeat

chest pains

immune suppression

infertility

birth defects

kidney/brain damage

Alzheimer's disease

anaemia

anxiety

sensitive tongue

metallic taste in mouth

MS symptoms

allergies

Any amount of metals in the body will have a negative effect on your health and your mental functioning, it is just that some people can tolerate more than others. Those who already suffer from allergies have a very low tolerance to toxins and metals. They cannot detox the metals well and therefore suffer more acute symptoms.

We all have a certain amount of metal that has deposited into our body tissues, so it is generally a good idea to, first and foremost, make sure that your mercury fillings are safely exchanged for less harmful ones (*see Useful Addresses, page 169*), and then to help the body detox by taking nutritional supplements that can bind and remove the toxins.

Supplements that help bind mercury and other metals so that they can leave the body are kelp, selenium (mercury, cadmium), zinc (lead, cadmium, mercury), iron (cadmium), vitamin C (lead, cadmium) and vitamin E (lead, cadmium and mercury). Also useful are the amino acids L-cysteine and glutathione. Many companies offer combination products that help detoxify the body from metals.

In summary, there is a lot you can do to support your body. We have looked at some factors that can be detrimental to health or even induce stress by their mere presence in your system.

Let's now look in more detail at supplements, including food, herbs, vitamins and minerals, that can support body, mind and emotions.

CHAPTER SIX

The holistic first aid kit

Many years ago when the term 'stress' was initially coined, it referred only to a mental or emotional overload that resulted in distress. Once stress was to do with grief, being overworked, having emotional problems or getting a divorce, but today we have to include the effects of noxious radiation and poisons in our environment.

The world around us has been under increasing attack from toxic fumes and substances. Heavy metals like lead, cadmium and mercury rain down on us, while poisonous fumes from industrial sites, exhaust fumes from cars and smoke from other people's cigarettes get into our lungs. Industrial heavy metals and car fumes are swept into the ground, but they come back up in the plants we eat. On top of that, we are also exposed to an increasing number of artificial electromagnetic fields and to radiation from a variety of sources, from X-ray machines to carelessly maintained nuclear power stations.

With all this environmental stress, it is particularly important to give the body a hand in ridding itself of these toxins. As already mentioned, a number of vitamins and minerals are very effective in binding toxins and transporting them out of the body. Lead can be discharged with zinc, vitamin C and vitamin E; cadmium with iron, zinc, vitamin C and E; and mercury with zinc and vitamin E. This chapter will give you information about other supplements you can take to help your body and mind cope better with stress. I have given you a short description of the function and effects of each remedy, be it vitamin, mineral or oil.

You will notice that hardly any of the supplements have a recommendation for the correct dosage. The reason for this is that there is no such thing as a correct dosage. Naturally, you can simply go by what it says on the bottle. Or, if you have the time, you can refer to some of the books that are mentioned in the Further Reading section (*see page 163*) to get an idea how much you should use. If you go by what it says on the bottle, you are definitely not going to take too much, but you may very well take too little to get an effect. This means that you may be spending a lot of money on supplements which are not working, when all you need is double the dose!

If you are unsure whether you need to increase the dosage, you have several options. You can either see a qualified nutritionist who will advise you of the right dosage, or you can go and see a kinesiologist who will be able to quickly test one of your muscles to find out what quantities your body needs. You will find contact addresses at the back of the book.

Yet another way of finding out exactly what your body needs is to send in a hair or nail sample to a laboratory and have it tested to see which minerals, vitamins or amino acids you are short of. A health kinesiologist will also be able to test for these nutrients and can also check which flower essences or aromatherapy oils would be right for you.

If you are having problems with your digestion or if you want to avoid the fillers in tablets or the alcohol in tinctures, you can also have remedies that are made with live water which has been magnetically imprinted with the signature of herbs, flower essences and homoeopathic remedies. That way, you avoid the sugar in homoeopathic pills as well. Each remedy is tailor-made for your particular case with the help of your hair or nail sample. The magnetised water is of excellent quality and has an unlimited shelf life and the individual array of signatures tunes into your particular health system. (*For further information, see Useful Addresses, page 168.*)

Vitamins, minerals and amino acids

To combat stress, it is essential to boost the immune system and to control blood sugar levels. The following vitamins and minerals help in reducing stress, controlling blood sugar levels and preventing oxidative damage.

Vitamins

Vitamin A

Vitamin A helps with eye disorders, skin problems and anti-body activity. It is essential for the management of cell growth and multiplication. It has been shown to fight infection and enhance immunity, and its ability as a cancer-fighting agent is well established. Insufficient levels of vitamin A can lead to alterations in the skin and mucous membranes and may even contribute to pre-cancerous conditions.

Vitamin A is found in green and yellow vegetables, and the best way of getting sufficient amounts of this immune-enhancing vitamin is to eat lots of those vegetables! The two major forms of vitamin A are retinol, which is provided in food of animal origin such as liver, milk, cheese, butter and egg yolks, and beta-carotene, a natural plant source, which is converted into vitamin A by the body as needed.

If you want to supplement your diet with vitamin A, take it together with vitamin C. Don't exceed 5,000 IU of vitamin A when you are pregnant, as larger quantities can cause reproductive hazards or birth defects. Beta-carotene poses no such risks.

Vitamin B complex

B vitamins help maintain healthy functioning of the nervous system and reduce the effects of stress. They convert carbohydrates into glucose, which the body 'burns' to produce energy. These vitamins are also essential for the metabolism of fats and proteins and for the maintenance of muscle tone in the gastrointestinal tract, as well as healthy digestive function.

All B-complex vitamins are water-soluble. This means that any excess is naturally excreted from the body, not stored, making continual replacement vital. B vitamins are easily destroyed by cooking and refining foods. Alcohol, coffee or tea consumption, as well as heavy perspiration, also result in the loss of certain B vitamins. Oestrogen, insecticides, sleeping pills and sulpha drugs create an environment in the digestive tract which can destroy B vitamins.

If you are working under stress or are a generally nervous person, you may need significantly higher doses of the B-complex vitamins.

Vitamin B1 (thiamine) helps convert blood sugar into energy and is a component of key metabolic reactions in the heart, in nerve tissues and in the production of new cells. Alcohol is particularly damaging to B1.

Vitamin B2 (riboflavin) works with an enzyme to help create energy and to inhibit free radical damage to the body. It is a strong antioxidant and necessary for iron absorption. Alcohol and a number of different types of drugs, including tranquillisers, destroy B2.

Vitamin B3 (niacin) aids in the production of energy in the cells, promotes mental and physical health, assists in regulating blood sugar levels and help to reduce high cholesterol.

Vitamin B5 (pantothenic acid) is crucial for healthy adrenal glands and hormone production. It is also needed for healthy digestion and for production of antibodies.

Vitamin B6 (pyridoxine) is critical to the normal functioning of essential enzymes and also helps keep the brain and nervous system functioning correctly.

Vitamin B12 (cyanocobalamin) is necessary for red blood cell formation and normal growth, for fertility and during pregnancy, and for building immunity and treating certain degenerative diseases (AIDS, cancer, MS and osteoarthritis). It is also used therapeutically for various mental and nervous disorders. Recently B12 has become a popular treatment for boosting energy and counteracting allergens.

Folic acid

Folic acid, one of the B vitamins, is crucial in pregnancy to ensure healthy development of the foetus, but is equally important when you are stressed. A deficiency can bring up symptoms such as irritability, tiring easily and an overall feeling of weakness. Folic acid also appears to be beneficial in reducing the damaging effects of smoking on the lungs.

Biotin enhances the body's immune system, so increasing its ability to fight a variety of diseases, including yeast infections. It also counteracts depression, exhaustion and muscle pain.

Choline is helpful for dealing with major nerve, psychiatric and infectious diseases. It improves mood and memory. Continued use of high doses of choline may cause a B6 deficiency.

Inositol is a complex form of fatty acid and is a natural tranquilliser which alleviates anxiety and promotes sleep.

PABA (para-aminobenzoic acid) occurs in conjunction with folic acid. It is produced by friendly colonic flora and is stored in the tissues. Lack of PABA can cause constipation, depression, digestive problems, fatigue, headaches, irritability and nervousness. Continued supplementation in doses higher than 30 mg is not recommended, unless under the care of a health practitioner, as it can be toxic.

Vitamin C

Vitamin C, also known as ascorbic acid, is a water-soluble substance which must be obtained from dietary sources. It helps form red blood cells, aids in the prevention of haemorrhaging and enhances fine bone and tooth formation. Vitamin C is also necessary for the functioning of other essential nutrients in the body. Intestinal absorption of iron is significantly increased by sufficient levels of vitamin C. It has been clinically proven to substantially decrease the intensity of colds and to help in preventing cancer. An adequate amount of vitamin C is vital for the creation of adrenalin in the adrenal glands. Adrenal ascorbic acid is quickly used up in times of stress and it is therefore important to replenish it regularly.

Take vitamin C in divided doses throughout the day to ensure consistent levels in the blood, as it is quickly excreted from the body. Take between 1,000 and 3,000 mg when you are stressed. If you get diarrhoea it means that you have exceeded your optimum level. Simply reduce your intake by 500 mg.

Vitamin E

Vitamin E is indispensable to all oxygen-breathing life and is an intricate component of energy production. It is fat-soluble and is made up of several substances called tocopherols. It is a powerful antioxidant which plays a vital role in the cellular respiration of all muscles, particularly cardiac and skeletal. It enables these muscles and associated nerves to operate with less oxygen, thus enhancing their endurance and stamina. Sufficient levels of vitamin E are essential for healthy neuro-logical functioning – a deficiency can often cause nerve damage. Vitamin E improves blood flow by dilating blood vessels, inhibits blood clotting, transports nutrients to cells, assists eye focus, promotes healing of wounds and reduces scarring, and protects the body against damage from environ-mental pollutants.

Vitamin E can be derived from food sources such as whole-grain cereals, all raw seeds and nuts, eggs, vegetables (especially leafy greens) and cold-pressed vegetable oils. As a supplement, take it together with selenium (*see page 145*).

Minerals

Calcium

Calcium is the most plentiful mineral in the body, with about 99 per cent stored in the bones and teeth. Calcium is a lifelong dietary requirement, necessary for muscle contractions, nerve transmission, immune system maintenance, regular heartbeat and the production of biological energy. Calcium also safe-guards the body against cardiovascular disease by reducing high blood pressure and lowering cholesterol, thus reducing the risk of heart attacks and strokes. When given together with magnesium, calcium can reduce nervousness, irritability, insomnia and headaches, and can also prevent premenstrual tension and osteoporosis.

Calcium should be taken with meals as the acidic environ-ment of the stomach enhances calcium absorption. It should also be taken together with magnesium and ideally vitamin D in order to ensure optimum absorption.

Chromium

This is an essential mineral if you cannot stop eating sweets and sugary things when you are stressed. Chromium is essen-tial for normal insulin functioning, helps decrease body fat and lowers cholesterol levels.

Use the picolinate or nicotinate preparations of chromium and take 400–500 mcg a day, divided up into two dosages taken before lunch and before dinner.

Magnesium

Magnesium is a vital element of the body, concentrated primarily in bones and within each cell. This major mineral is essential for every important biological function, including glucose metabolism, the production and balance of cellular energy and the manufacturing of nucleic acids and proteins. Magnesium helps preserve the electrical balance of cells and is essential for membrane integrity, proper muscle contrac-tion, nerve conduction, regular heartbeat and venous health. It is also essential for calcium absorption. It suppresses parathyroid hormone (PTH), which extracts calcium from the bones, and stimulates calcitonin, a hormone which increases and maintains calcium stores in the bones. Magnesium also helps nerves to relax after having been stimulated by calcium, thus promoting a healthy balance of muscle and nerve function.

A magnesium deficiency can result in confusion, fatigue,

loss of appetite, loss of co-ordination, nausea, tremors and vomiting.

Take two parts calcium with one part magnesium with meals or buy a supplement which already combines both minerals and, ideally, also contains vitamin D.

Selenium

Selenium is an important mineral which works together with vitamin E to carry out many metabolic functions, including normal growth and fertility. It is a powerful antioxidant and anti-cancer nutrient. It is known to guard the body from numerous disorders, including arteriosclerosis, coronary artery disease, heart attacks and strokes.

Selenium can be found in many vegetables, such as broccoli, cauliflower, garlic, onions and radishes. However, the selenium content in food is dependent on the amount of selenium in the soil where the food is grown, so chances are you need to supplement it as our soils today are generally of poor quality.

Zinc

Zinc is vital to a healthy immune system because it speeds the healing of wounds and assists thymus function. It is an important element in the healthy absorption and function of vitamins, especially the B-complex vitamins. It is involved in digestion and metabolism, tissue growth, maintenance and repair.

Zinc is destroyed when food is processed and low levels of zinc are common today. Zinc deficiencies lead to abnormalities of sense and perception (loss of smell or taste), increased risk of infection, lethargy, malfunctioning sex glands and poor appetite. If you eat lots of fibre, this will deplete your zinc levels, as will eating little meat or being on a calorie-reduced diet. Zinc supplements are important, especially for vegetarians. Take up to a maximum of 150 mg a day.

Amino acids

GABA

GABA stands for gamma-aminobutyric acid and is a non-essential amino acid, formed from glutamic acid, which maintains healthy brain function and helps balance brain chemistry. Called the 'anxiety amino acid', GABA acts as a major inhibitory neurotransmitter to induce relaxation and produce a sense of tranquillity and calmness.

GABA has been shown to play a crucial role in the regulation of anxiety and panic. Researchers believe that it influences the brain by slowing the activity of neurons associated with acute agitation which consequently helps lower blood pressure, stop excessive perspiration and soothe palpitations and a 'racing' mind.

GABA can be taken as a natural tranquilliser without fear of addiction or negative side-effects.

L-carnitine

L-carnitine is an amino acid utilised by the body for proper energy and fat metabolism. As it helps convert fatty acids into energy, it also aids the liver. Carnitine can be produced by the body in the presence of sufficient levels of B1, B6, iron and lysine. It is readily available in meat, especially dark turkey and red meats, so vegetarians are more prone to develop a deficiency. Carnitine has also been shown to increase the effectiveness of vitamins C and E.

A study found that alcohol mars the body's ability to manufacture carnitine, thus compromising fatty-acid conversion. When alcohol or high-fat diets are consumed, greater levels of carnitine are required to manage the excess toxins produced. Carnitine production is also hampered by crash diets, environmental pollutants, prolonged fatigue and inefficient digestive function.

L-carnitine supplements help prevent levels from dropping and keep fatty-acid deposits from accumulating in the liver, as well as in the heart and other muscles. Other advantages of taking L-carnitine are that it helps regulate heart arrhythmias, increases resistance to stress and supplies greater physical stamina.

L-cysteine

Cysteine is a water-soluble sulphur amino acid that is a biochemical powerhouse. Its most exciting trait is its ability to help the body rid itself of harmful toxic chemicals such as mercury, as well as toxins which occur in cancer treatments. In itself, cysteine is also used in combating cancer.

Apart from helping with metal toxicity, cysteine also plays a role in energy metabolism and has been successfully used in the treatment of hair loss in women, psoriasis and bacterial infection.

L-glutathione

There are virtually no living organisms – animal or plant – whose cells don't contain some glutathione. Scientists believe that glutathione was essential to the very development of life on Earth. The liver, spleen, kidneys, stomach lining, pancreas and eyes contain the greatest amount of glutathione. This decreases with age.

Glutathione plays four primary roles in the body. It protects against powerful man-made oxidants, it helps the liver detoxify poisonous chemicals, it supports immune function and protects the integrity of red blood cells. It is able to bind and remove metals such as lead, mercury, arsenic and cadmium.

Fatty acids

Omega 3

Omega-3 oils help lower LDL cholesterol, raise good HDL cholesterol and lower triglycerides by preventing blood cells from sticking together on arterial walls. They help the brain work more efficiently, protect liver and kidneys, regulate irregular heartbeat and normalise blood pressure if it is too high.

Omega-3 oils must be supplied in the diet. Natural fish oils are rich in them, but if you are not keen on fish oil, they are also found in flaxseed oil (also known as linseed oil) or pumpkin seed. Fish rich in omega-3 fatty acids are halibut, salmon and mackerel.

Omega 6

Omega-6 fatty acids are essential for a strong immune system and hormonal balance. They also help reduce inflammatory processes. Deficiency can lead to eczema, psoriasis, hair loss, infertility and weight gain as well as behavioural and circulatory problems. Smoking, alcohol, viral infections and eating a lot of saturated fats can cause a deficiency.

Supplementing your diet with evening primrose oil or starflower oil (borage oil) will supply the vital gamma-linolenic acid (GLA) which the body needs, particularly under stress.

A supplement that combines both omega 3 and omega 6 is blackcurrant oil.

Healing herbs

Herbs are highly effective and just as potent as pharmaceutical drugs. This means that you should not take any herbal remedies when you are on other medically prescribed drugs as the herbs can interact negatively with pharmaceuticals.

Herbal remedies should never be taken for longer than seven weeks continuously. Avoid them when you are pregnant or breastfeeding. If in doubt, see a professional herbalist or health kinesiologist to check out which herb and which dosage is the most appropriate for you (*see Useful Addresses, page 169*).

Feverfew

Feverfew is valuable for a variety of nervous problems and is specifically used for highly nervous people who are oversensitive to pain and prone to sudden fits of irritability or anger. Research and clinical trials have shown feverfew to be also highly effective for headaches and migraines. It acts as a tonic to the nervous system, relaxing tension and lifting depression.

Gingko biloba

The subject of a great many studies and trials, gingko is highly effective as a vasodilator, opening constricted blood vessels to promote normalised circulation to the brain and central nervous system. This has been proven to reverse such problems as depression, fatigue, headache, short-term memory loss and vertigo. It is also effective for the early stages of Alzheimer's disease. If you have problems concentrating or remembering, this is the herb for you.

If you can get a tincture, this is preferable to tablets. Take it in water as prescribed on the bottle. If you don't get any effects, double the dosage.

Hops

Herbalists have long used hops as a standard remedy for soothing nerves, anxiety, excitability, irritability, tension headaches and nervous gastrointestinal complaints such as irritable bowel syndrome. Hops also help promote sleep and the hop acids stimulate the production of digestive fluids, help neutralise an over-acid stomach and remedy indigestion.

The calming effect of hops usually occurs within 20 to 40 minutes of taking the supplement. Hops are usually employed in conjunction with valerian and have been shown in controlled clinical trials to be equally effective as benzodi-azepine drugs.

You should not use hops if you are prone to depression.

Kelp

Kelp is a valuable sea vegetable which nourishes and supports the glandular system, particularly the thyroid. It is best known as a popular natural remedy for treating an underac-tive thyroid. Kelp enhances kidney function and corrects hormone imbalances. Its rich supply of nutrients improves digestion and respiration, helps reduce the effects of stress upon the body, increases immunity and promotes general well-being. It is rich in iodine salts and amino acids which enhance thyroid function and stimulate metabolism, as well as assisting nervous system functions. It promotes greater energy and endurance and increases circulation, especially to the brain.

Passionflower

Traditionally, passionflower has been used for insomnia and disturbed sleep patterns. Today, its sedative, tranquillising and sleep-inducing qualities have been confirmed in studies, and the herb is widely used for anxiety, hyperactivity in children, hypertension, irritability, nervous tachycardia, nervous tension and panic.

Do not use passionflower remedies during pregnancy.

St John's Wort

St John's Wort relaxes muscle spasms, expels phlegm, stimulates the immune system, calms and strengthens nerves and promotes urine flow. The herb contains hypericin, a substance which has antiviral and antidepressive properties and has been used successfully as a natural antidepressant. Studies show that hypericin reduces levels of anxiety and depression and increases levels of dopamine and serotonin, which elevate mood.

Valerian

Valerian has been used throughout history as a natural sedative and sleep aid. It is non-addictive and its effects are not increased with alcohol consumption. It can be used as a healthy alternative to Valium. Results from extensive research conducted in Germany and Switzerland validate the use of valerian for promoting restful sleep, improving the quality of sleep and reducing blood pressure. Further benefits of this herb are reduction of nervous tension, aggression, irritability, depression, fatigue, headaches, palpitations, panic, sweating and tremors. The advantage of valerian over pharmaceutical sleeping products is that it improves sleep without the drowsy, lethargic side-effects the next morning. Valerian is also high in calcium and magnesium.

Flower remedies

Today, there are a great number of different flower essences on the market and in my book *Inner Happiness* I have given a fuller account of them than I have here. In the context of stress management, I have picked out a number of Bach Flower Remedies for you, as these are most readily available in health-food shops.

Bach Flower Remedies are best taken in water. For great stress, take 20 drops in a little water and sip the water slowly. Repeat this dosage three times a day. Stop taking it as soon as the stress has abated.

Bach Flower Remedies are safe to take with other medication and can also be taken when you are pregnant. Combine as many remedies as you want.

Agrimony
For those who hide their troubles behind humour. They go to great lengths to avoid arguments and may use alcohol or drugs to stimulate themselves and help cope with pain or anxiety. They are oversensitive to ideas and influences.

Aspen
For those with vague fears of the unknown, a sense of foreboding, nightmares or terror of approaching misfortune for no apparent reason. They are often afraid to talk about these fears to other people.

Centaury
For kind people who find it hard to say 'no', being over-anxious to please and serve others. They work harder on other people's behalf than on their own.

Cherry Plum
For those fearful of losing control of their body, mind or emotions and expressing uncontrollable anger and other impulses which may cause them to harm themselves or others, including suicidal tendencies.

Crab apple

For those who feel they need cleansing, have low self-esteem and concentrate obsessively on one shameful aspect of themselves.

Elm

For diligent people who are doing good work but who feel overburdened or over-extended at times, which causes depression and despondency.

Gentian

For those who are easily discouraged, in whom small setbacks can cause depression, despondency and self-doubt, even though generally they do well.

Holly

For people who are overcome by negative emotions such as anger, jealousy, envy and suspicion. They suffer greatly inside, often when there is no real cause.

Hornbeam

For those who feel they need strengthening and help physically or mentally to bear the burden life has placed upon their shoulders. For that 'Monday morning feeling', not feeling up to facing the coming day and the pressures of everyday life.

Impatiens

For those who think and act quickly and who want everything done without delay. They are often happier working or being alone so that they can go at their own speed, as they are often irritated by others who do things more slowly.

Larch

For despondent and despairing people who do not consider themselves as good as others. Even though they may be perfectly able, they lack confidence and expect failure, so that often they do not try hard enough to succeed and their view of themselves becomes a self-fulfilling prophecy.

THE HOLISTIC FIRST AID KIT • 153

Olive

For those suffering complete mental and physical exhaustion. Their daily life seems hard and without joy. They are worn out from mental or physical ordeals and suffering.

Pine

For despondent and despairing people who blame themselves and feel guilty. Even when they are satisfied, they are not satisfied with their efforts or results and feel they could have done better. They work hard and suffer a great deal from the faults they attach to themselves, even claiming responsibility for mistakes which are not theirs.

Rescue Remedy

A must for your briefcase or handbag, if you are stressed! Rescue Remedy or, as it is sometimes called, Recovery Remedy, is a combination of Impatiens, Clematis, Rock Rose, Cherry Plum and Star of Bethlehem.

Rock Rose

For those experiencing fright, panic, terror or hysteria. A remedy for emergencies.

Star of Bethlehem

For great distress and unhappiness following some kind of shock such as bad news, the death of a loved one or an accident.

Sweet chestnut

For those in despair who feel that the anguish is so great it is unbearable. They have reached the limits of their endurance and there is nothing left but dark despair.

Walnut

For those who need to break links with the past and to adjust to a new phase (for example moving house, changing jobs), to balance emotions in transition periods (for example starting school, puberty, marriage, menopause) or to come to terms with the death of a loved one. The remedy also offers protection from outside influences which may cause a person to stray from their chosen path.

White chestnut
For those with persistent unwanted thoughts and ideas which, though thrown out, return when there is not sufficient interest in the present to occupy the mind. For those with mental arguments, preoccupation or obsessive thoughts which cause mental torture and an inability to relax or concentrate fully on work or leisure.

Willow
For those who feel bitter or resentful about their misfortune and, as a result, take less interest in the things in life they used to enjoy doing. They are despondent and feel that life is unjust and unfair.

Aromatherapy oils

Aromatherapy oils are essentially concentrated from the volatile oils that give herbs their aromatic taste and smell. Volatile oils are composed of a great number of different chemical constituents. They are antiseptic and enhance the function of the immune system. Many oils have anti-inflammatory and antispasmodic properties, others bring relief if the digestive tract is inflamed or irritated, and still others help to clear phlegm or excess fluid from the body.

The reason why aromatherapy oils are particularly beneficial for treating stress-related problems is because they not only exert their beneficial effect on the body, but also reach the brain and nervous system as you inhale them. When we breathe in the aroma of the oils, we stimulate nerve endings in the upper part of the nose which in turn carry nerve impulses to the brain. As the oils are inhaled, tiny molecules are also taken into the lungs and absorbed into the bloodstream. Similarly, when an aromatherapy oil is rubbed into the skin, this relays messages to the underlying tissues and muscles, which in turn has an effect on the nervous system and especially the pituitary gland which regulates the action of all other endocrine glands. This is why aromatherapy oils can substantially help hormonal problems as well as relieving stress and furthering relaxation.

How to use the oils

Aromatherapy oils are very powerful concentrates which have to be used carefully, so please don't go and dab them on as perfume! Avoid using them near the eyes, and never take them internally or apply them undiluted to the skin. If you have sensitive skin, dilute an oil as described below and try it on a small area of skin for two to three days in a row to make sure you don't react unfavourably to it. It is also best to avoid aromatherapy oils when you are pregnant, unless you are advised by a qualified aromatherapist.

To dilute oils, use a base oil such as sweet almond oil, apricot kernel or avocado oil. Use 50 ml of base oil and add 25 drops of essential oil. If you want to combine several aromatherapy oils, that is fine, but do not exceed the overall 25 drops. This means, for example, that if you want to use bergamot and chamomile oils in your base, add 12 drops of one and 13 drops of the other. If your skin is particularly sensitive, reduce the number of drops that you add to the base to 12.

You can use the oils in a variety of ways:

- Rub a little onto your wrist or neck.

- Add 5–10 drops to your bathwater and soak in it for about 15 minutes.

- Add 5–10 drops in a vaporiser to scent the atmosphere of your room.

- Add 10 drops to a spray bottle with water and spray it around the room.

- Put 2–4 drops in a bowl of hot (not boiling) water and

breathe in the air with a towel over your head for five minutes.

Soothing oils

Below, you will find a list of oils which are particularly helpful for stress problems. You won't need all these oils in your first aid kit, though! I just wanted to give you a wide choice in case you are having problems getting any of them. Choose ones that appeal to you – use your intuition.

Basil

If the smell of the basil oil is not too sweet for you, you will find it an excellent oil to use for stress. It helps calm you down and strengthens the nerves, clears and stimulates the mind and lifts the spirits. It is refreshing when you feel tired, yet calming when you feel anxious. It is a very useful oil for the relief of headaches, migraines, exhaustion, indigestion and muscle pain. When you are feeling weak and vulnerable, basil strengthens and revitalises.

Bergamot

Bergamot oil acts as a gentle antidepressant. It helps lift the spirits and has a refreshing effect if you feel down and weepy during stressful times or if you suffer from PMS. Bergamot also improves mental clarity and alertness and sharpens the senses. It can be used to relieve built-up stress and tension, calming and relaxing the muscles.

Bergamot can increase the skin's sensitivity to sunlight or ultraviolet light from sunbeds.

Chamomile

Chamomile oil has a calming, soothing effect on the central nervous system which is helpful for relieving anxiety, depression, insomnia and emotional hypersensitivity. It also diffuses anger, hysteria, choleric temper, moodiness, nightmares and symptoms related to shock. According to researchers at Cambridge University, inhaling chamomile oil causes individuals to shift from describing images in negative terms to describing them in positive terms. Inhaling the oil can be particularly helpful for those with nervous and allergic asthmatic conditions that are exacerbated during times of stress.

Clary sage

Clary sage is an effective relaxant with sedative properties that are to some degree aphrodisiac and antidepressant. It is useful for insomnia and feelings of panic, and is also recommended for stomach problems such as dyspepsia (indigestion) and flatulence, as well as headaches and vertigo. The oil's high ester content explains its effectiveness as an antispasmodic, capable of reducing tension in stressful situations, as well as its antifungal properties. Be careful with clary sage oil, though, as it can cause headaches when used in confined spaces. Overuse may actually raise blood pressure and cause dizziness. Avoid during pregnancy.

Geranium

Geranium balances and enhances your mood and emotional outlook. It has long been used for its effect on the psyche. Research shows that it affects the adrenal cortex, which helps to explain its ability to relieve depression, nervousness, emotional weariness and symptoms associated with PMS and the menopause.

Hyssop

Hyssop oil helps relieve anxiety, tension, exhaustion and depression and is generally supportive in times of stress. Use it in a vaporiser and it will help clear your mind and steady your nerves when you have to study for an exam.

Lavender

Lavender oil is considered an emotional balancer. It lifts the spirits and acts as a tonic to the nervous system. It restores strength and vitality when you suffer from nervous exhaustion and relaxes the digestive tract, soothing away colic related to tension and anxiety. Inhalation of the essential oil has a relaxing effect on body and mind and acts on physical symptoms such as tension, headaches, migraines, trembling, palpitations and insomnia.

Lemon balm

Also known as melissa oil, lemon balm calms and slows the heart, eases palpitations and reduces high blood pressure. It can be used to calm nerves and anxiety, release tension and tension headaches and relieve insomnia. While it has relaxant properties, it also acts as a tonic and is a good remedy for stress-related indigestion. Massaged into the lower abdomen, it relieves period pains and generally relaxes muscles and eases tension.

Neroli

Neroli oil acts as a natural sedative to calm nervous tension, relieve anxiety and promote restful sleep. This oil is recommended for a variety of psychological problems ranging from depression and insomnia to stage fright and performance nerves. However, it can also be used to relieve more serious conditions such as hypersensitivity, PMS, emotional shock or trauma, feelings of desperation and even the inability to confront emotional fears. In addition, neroli oil has antispasmodic and hypotensive (lowering blood pressure) properties which help to restore the heart's natural rhythm and improve palpitations.

Pine

Use pine oil in the morning to wake yourself up, invigorate your mind and enliven your senses. It can also be used later on in the day when you feel exhausted, anxious and generally stressed, as it has a calming and refreshing quality to it. It is also warming and strengthening and stimulates the circulation in winter.

Rosemary

Rosemary oil has an uplifting effect and helps dispel depression. It awakens the senses and has a generally stimulating effect. It is a tonic to the nerves, heart, circulation and digestion. It is excellent when you feel tired or lethargic or when your concentration and memory have suffered because of stress.

Help for exhausted glands

When you have been under stress for a long time, your glands will have borne the brunt of the onslaught. A gland is an organ that secretes hormones into the bloodstream and causes a physiological change. The thyroid, adrenal and thymus glands all have important and specific functions in maintaining health and well-being in the body. Organs such as the heart, liver and spleen can also be classified as glands, even though they do not secrete hormones.

In the past, our diet contained much more offal such as liver, kidneys and heart than it does now. With the recent crises in the meat industry, we have become very wary of eating any inner organs for fear of contracting BSE. Also, it is no longer fashionable to eat offal and few restaurants have it on the menu now. However, when we are stressed out and running on empty, our glands need support. This can be given in the form of bovine glands. It goes without saying that this tissue concentrate comes from a reputable supplier, using only healthy cattle that are grass fed and have not been subjected to growth hormones and antibiotic medication. The best way of processing this tissue is lyophilisation, where the gland is trimmed of fat and then quickly freeze-dried. (For vegetarians, there are herbal alternatives, as detailed later.)

The thyroid

The thyroid gland sits like a bow-tie around the front part of the neck. One of its main functions is to control the rate of metabolism. It is a vital link in the endocrine system and even a small decline in its hormonal output can have a serious effect on the metabolism levels. If your thyroxin output is too low due to stress, you can develop the following symptoms:

depression

anxiety

deteriorating memory

hair loss

weight gain

loss of libido

fatigue

cold hands and feet

A simple way of checking whether your thyroid needs support is to use the axillary temperature test. Do the following:

- Place a thermometer under your arm as soon as you wake up. (Use a traditional glass thermometer. They are more reliable than digital ones.)

- Keep it in position for 10 minutes. Do not talk or move during this time.

- Check your temperature.

- Do the same test for four consecutive days. Try to do it at the same time each day. Men can check their temperature on any four days. For women who are menstruating, their temperature is best measured on days two, three, four and five of their period. Before puberty and after menopause, choose any days.

The normal temperature range is 97.8°F–98.2°F or 36.6°C–36.8°C.

If your average temperature measurements are *below* the above figures and if you display any of the symptoms described above, you could be suffering from an underfunctioning thyroid.

If you want to have your thyroid function checked, you can have standard laboratory tests done through your GP or, if you are willing to pay for it yourself, get the tests done privately, as you will be given the results personally. Make sure that not only the free thyroxine (T4) levels are tested, but also the thyroid-stimulating hormone (TSH) levels. If T4 levels are at the lower end of the normal range and TSH levels at the higher end, this is an indication of reduced thyroid function, even though the laboratory will possibly declare it as normal.

If you are averse to taking animal products to help the thyroid, you can also take kelp or herbal products that support the thyroid (*see Useful Addresses, page 173, for suppliers*).

The adrenals

Also very important are the adrenal glands, which sit like little hats on the kidneys. When you are stressed, they produce adrenalin, which helps release more sugar into the bloodstream to increase energy levels so you can cope better with the stress. However, this energy boost doesn't last long, and if already overstretched adrenals continue to be stimulated, they become exhausted.

Symptoms of fatigued adrenals can include the following:

tiredness

listlessness

feeling physically weak

hypoglycaemia

mental confusion

menstrual disturbances

loss of body hair in women

low blood pressure

In order to support the adrenals, it is important to make sure that you have a sufficient intake of vitamins A, C, B complex and zinc (*see pages 140–5*). Again, you can take either a bovine extract or you can use herbal remedies.

The thymus

The third very important gland in the body is the thymus. It plays a central role in the maintenance of a healthy immune system. It is situated behind the breastbone and produces T-lymphocytes, which are essential in helping the body fight infections such as candida and other fungi, hepatitis B, parasites, herpes simplex or Epstein Barr. If you suffer from an infection caused by these organisms, or if you want to combat allergies such as asthma or hayfever, you may find that you need to support the thymus gland with glandular extract or with herbs. Here, too, an adequate supply of antioxidant nutrients is important. Make sure you get enough vitamins A, C, E, B complex, zinc and selenium.

Conclusion

Although stress is not something we usually welcome into our life, it can nevertheless have a very positive function in that it helps us grow as a person. If you have started using the exercises in this book, you will have already noticed yourself becoming stronger and more resilient to events that used to upset you in the past.

There is no law that says you *have* to be stressed in certain situations. There are always at least another three better options for dealing with a problem than reacting with stress. Learning how to deal with life's ups and downs in a constructive way is an ongoing process, so have this book at hand for a while longer. Exercises which you haven't looked at yet might become relevant to you tomorrow.

Successful stress management is not handed down to you by a benign celestial force – it is the result of taking positive action. In the end, it is *your* responsibility whether you get your stress sorted out or not. No one else can do it for you. Taking that responsibility can be one of the best things you have ever done in your life.

Further Reading

David Allen, *Getting Things Done: How to achieve stress-free productivity*, Piatkus Books, 2002
This offers practical ways of time management. The author teaches you how to apply the 'do it, delegate it, defer it, drop it' principle to empty your 'in' tray and how to handle e-mail, paperwork and unexpected demands more quickly.

Dr F. Batmanghelidj, *Your Body's Many Cries for Water: A revolutionary natural way to prevent illness and restore good health*, Tagman Press, 2000
The author, a medical doctor, explains how he discovered the healing powers of plain water. He successfully treated a great number of people with problems such as high blood pressure, intestinal disorders, stress, allergies and many more ailments by prescribing water. He claims that most illnesses can be prevented and cured by drinking enough water.

Beryl Crane, *Reflexology: An Illustrated Guide*, Element Books, 1998
Practical advice for self-help, with step-by-step photographs to illustrate the techniques needed. Anatomy of the foot, hand and ear included. Self-treatment and basic techniques explained clearly, with a comprehensive reference section.

Sybil Evans with Sherry Suib Cohen, *Hot Buttons: How to resolve conflict and cool everyone down*, Piatkus Books, 2002
This is the book for you if you have a tendency to explode or lash out when things don't go your way. It outlines a straight-forward five-step process to help you resolve arguments in a healthier and more constructive way.

Ann Gillanders, *The Family Guide to Reflexology*, Gaia Books, 1998
Treatments for all ages, from childhood colic to common adult ailments like asthma, migraine, PMT, back pain and IBS, from family first aid to caring for the elderly, with clear guidelines.

Lynne McTaggart, *The Field: The quest for the secret force of the universe*, HarperCollins, 2001
An outstanding book which collects research from eminent scientists who accidentally came across the Zero Point Field, a field of unimaginably large quantum energy in the space between things.

Penelope Ode, *The Complete Guide: Medicinal Herbs; Herbal remedies for common ailments*, Dorling Kindersley, 2000
An excellent guide with an A–Z of over 120 medicinal herbs and their applications. Contains instructions of how to use tinctures or capsules made from the various herbs.

Vera Peiffer, *Inner Happiness: Positive steps to feeling complete*, Piatkus Books, 2002
A comprehensive self-help guide for anyone who feels there is something missing from their lives. Contains instructions for simple muscle testing that will allow you to choose the right remedies to help you combat stress.

Vera Peiffer, *Positive Living: The complete guide to positive think-ing and personal success*, Piatkus Books, 2001
Effective strategies for dealing creatively with every aspect of your life, from work and health to relationships and emotional problems. Includes an A–Z of common problems with advice, affirmations and visualisations to help overcome each one.

Vera Peiffer, *Positively Single*, Thorsons, 1991
If you are stressed about being single, this is the book for you.
This practical guide shows you how to overcome the worries
and fears of being single, how to develop a more positive self-
image, make friends, develop new social skills and expand
your boundaries.

Jane Thurnell-Read, *Health Kinesiology: The muscle testing system
that talks to the body*, Able Publishing, 2002
An excellent guide that explains how muscle testing works and
how health kinesiologists can help you restore your health and
well-being.

Michael Van Straten, *Foods for Mind and Body: A complete guide
to the preventative and healing properties of food*, HarperCollins,
1997
A beautifully presented guide that explains which foods can
help you through various phases of your life. It also gives you
a food index with explanations about various groups of food
as well as an A–Z of common ailments and conditions that can
be prevented or cured by eating the right foods.

Useful Addresses

Acupressure (Shiatsu)

Pressure on acupoints helps vital energy to move freely in the body. It is applied with fingertips, thumbs or the heel of the hand to various parts of the body.

The Shiatsu Society (UK)
Eastlands Court
St Peter's Road
Rugby
Warwickshire
CV21 3QP
Tel.: 01788 555051
www.shiatsu.org

Acupuncture

Acupuncture involves the stimulation of acupuncture points with very fine needles in order to help the gland or organ that is connected with that point.

The British Acupuncture Council
63 Jeddo Road
London W12 9HQ
Tel. 020 87350400
Fax 020 87350404
www.acupuncture.org.uk

Alcohol problems

Alcoholics Anonymous
PO Box 1
Stonebow House
York
YO1 2NJ
Tel. 08457 697 555 (2 a.m.–10 p.m. every day)

Alcohol Concern
Tel. 020 7928 7377

Drinkline
Tel. 0800 917 8282
(9 a.m.–11 p.m. Mon–Fri, 6 p.m.–11 p.m. Sat/Sun)

Bach Flower Remedies

Contact the centre (below) for books by and about Edward
Bach. The centre also arranges courses and sells the Bach
Flower Remedies.

The Dr Edward Bach Centre
Mount Vernon
Sotwell
Wallingford
Oxon.
OX10 0PZ
Tel. 01491 834678
www.bachcentre.com

Flower essences

For a list of a great range of different flower essences, ask for
the full catalogue from:

The Nutri Centre
7 Park Crescent
London W1N 3HE
Information and order hotline: 020 7436 5122
www.nutricentre.com

Hair analysis for metal toxicity and mineral analysis

Omnilabs is continuously accredited by the Clinical Pathology Accreditation Scheme and has a quality manager to ensure the accuracy of their results. They are very helpful and will advise you over the phone what to send in if you want your mineral or metal toxicity levels checked.

Omnilabs Pathology Services
27 Harley Street
London W1G 9QP
Tel. 020 7908 7000

Hair analysis for preparation of individual remedies

If you want to have a remedy tailor-made for you, please contact me for a brochure. Remedies are made with live water and may contain homoeopathics, flower remedies or emotional light signatures to help you overcome your particular stress problem.

Vera Peiffer
10 Harley Street
London W1G 1PF
Tel. 020 7467 8497
www.vera-peiffer.com/health

Health kinesiology

With health kinesiology an indicator muscle is tested to identify stresses on the individual's energy system. Acupuncture points are held to bring the body back into balance and allergy checks are carried out, along with tests to ascertain which remedies are necessary to bring the body back into balance.

For a list of practitioners contact:

Health Kinesiology UK
Tel. 08707 655980
www.hk4health.com

For courses in health kinesiology, contact:

Ann Parker
44 Woodland Way
Old Tupton
Chesterfield
N. Derbys.
S42 6JA
Tel. 01246 862339
E-mail annparker@lineone.net

Herbalism

Herbalism is an ancient worldwide system of medicine using plants to prevent and cure disease.

The National Institute of Medical Herbalists
56 Longbrook Street
Exeter
Devon
EX4 6AH
Tel. 01392 426022
Fax 01392 498963
www.nimh.org.uk

Holistic dentistry

The British Society for Mercury-free Dentistry
221–223 Old Brompton Road
London SW5 0EA
Tel. 020 7370 0055
www.mercuryfree.co.uk

Homoeopathy

Homoeopathy is governed by the principle that agents which produce certain symptoms in health also cure those symptoms in disease and that the more a drug is diluted, the more powerful it becomes.

The Society of Homoeopaths
2 Artizan Road
Northampton
NN1 4HU
Tel. 01604 621400
Fax 01604 622622
www.homoeopathy.org.uk

Hypnotherapy

A very well-established and effective method of treating depressive illnesses which uses the hypnotic state to work through traumatic events in order to gain or regain confidence and self-esteem.

The Corporation of Advanced Hypnotherapy
PO Box 70
Southport
PR9 9HR
Tel./Fax 01704 576 285
www.abc-hypnotherapy.co.uk

Live water

For a catalogue of energised water devices for the house and for the handbag, contact:

Ultimate Water Ltd
1 Mayfield Avenue
London W4 1PN
Tel. 020 8400 9070
Fax 020 8995 0188
www.grander.co.uk

Nutrition

To find out about a nutritionist in your area, contact:

The Institute of Optimum Nutrition
Blades Court
Deodar Road
London SW15 2NU
Tel. 020 8877 9993
www.ion.ac.uk

Positive thinking

For simple and effective strategies for gaining greater confidence using visualisation, affirmations and other strategies to overcome stress, also a correspondence course, practical training and Positive Thinking counsellor's qualification, contact:

The Peiffer Foundation
39 Minniedale
Surbiton
Surrey
KT5 8DH
Tel. 020 8404 9774
www.vera-peiffer.com

Protection from mobile phone radiation

For a Cell-Plus device for your mobile phone which protects you from noxious effects:

Tel. 020 8823 9099
Fax 020 8823 9098
www.cell-plus.co.uk

Psychotherapy

The National Council of Psychotherapists was established in 1971 and offers a register of qualified members who work with different types of psychotherapy. The NCP also provides further training for practitioners.

The National Council of Psychotherapists (NCP)
PO Box 6072
Nottingham
NG6 9BW
Tel. 0115 913 1382
www.natcouncilofpsychotherapists.org.uk

Reflexology

An ancient Chinese and Indian diagnostic and therapeutic system in which the soles of the feet and sometimes the palms of the hands are massaged.

The British Reflexology Association
Monks Orchard
Whitbourne
Worcester
WR6 5RB
Tel. 01886 821207
www.britreflex.co.uk

Stopping smoking

Laser therapy is acupuncture using a painless 'soft' laser beam instead of needles. You may need several visits to stop.

The London Smoking Cessation Centre
Howard Chambers
Church Street
Enfield
Middlesex
EN2 6AJ
Tel. 020 8245 4769
www.quitsmokingnow.co.uk

Supplements: herbal tinctures

Ring Kinetic and ask them for a price list for their range of Nature's Answer products. These are made with very little or no alcohol.

Kinetic
Suite 419
258 Belsize Road
London NW6 4BT
Tel. 020 7435 5911

Thought field therapy

Devised by Dr Roger Callahan, a clinical psychologist, this method helps overcome trauma, physical pain, phobias, depression and a great number of other psychological problems by tapping acupuncture points, mainly on the face and on the hands. It works very well for jetlag too!

Dr Roger Callahan
78–816 Via Carmel
La Quinta, CA 92553
USA
Tel. 001 760 564 1925
www.tftrx.com

For courses in England, contact:

Robin Ellis
Rumwood
Horseheath
Cambridge
CB1 6QX
Tel. 01223 892596
e-mail robinellis@rumwood.demon.co.uk

Index

Note: page numbers in *italics* refer to diagrams and recipes.

action, constructive 26
activating the stress response
    13–15
acupressure 113–15, *114*
ADH *see* alcohol dehydrogenase
adrenal glands 159, 161
adrenal (stress) hormones 12,
    15–16
advantage takers 93
affirmations 77, 78
agrimony 151
alcohol consumption 52–5
    moderate 52–3
    problem signs 54
    reducing 54–5
    side effects of drinking too
        much 53–4
alcohol dehydrogenase (ADH)
    53
alcoholic units 52–3
allergies, dairy 129–32
amino acid supplements 146–7
anger 95–9
    dealing with angry people 96–8
    as fear 95
anger room technique 96
animal welfare 132
anticipation
    of stress 46
    of success 50–1
antioxidants 133
anxiety 146

aromatherapy oils 154–9
artificial sweeteners 125–6
ascorbic acid (vitamin C) 140,
    142–3
aspartame 125–6
aspen 151
assessing stress 35–42
attitudes
    to life 35
    to stress 9
avoidance strategies 2

Bach Flower Remedies 151–4
backstabbers 103–4
balance 11–12
    see also imbalance
basil oil 156
Batmanghelidj, Dr 129
behavioural signs of stress 22–4
beliefs, personal 35–6
belly breathing exercise 111–13
bergamot oil 156
beta-carotene 140
BHF *see* British Heart Foundation
biotin 142
blaming
    life in general 84
    yourself 82
bodily freezing 110–11
body support 108–37
    and dairy foods 129–32
    and mercury poisoning 134–7

nutritional supplements for
132–4
and physical self-sabotage
119–29
practical exercises and tips for
110–18
quick fixes for 109–10
body temperature 160
bones 129, 131
boredom 59
bosses, dealing with angry 96–8
boundaries/rules 91–5
brain 47
breakdowns 40
breathing
exercises 47, 70–1, 111–13
shallow 47
British Heart Foundation (BHF)
132
'build-up', stress 39
bullies, dealing with 102–3
busy states 38

calcium 129, 130–1, 143–4
calmatives
aromatherapy oils as 156–7,
158
dietary 118–19
herbal 149, 150
cancer, prostate 130
L-carnitine 146–7
carrier oils 155
case studies
learning to say no 61
managing families 94–5
managing fear 14–15, 21–2
managing impatience with
children 90–1
managing nausea 17
managing obsessive thoughts
24
managing poor memory 19
Cat Pose 115–16, *116*, 117–18
causes of stress 10
Celery and houmous 118–19
centaury 151
challenges 9, 59
chamomile oil 156–7
cherry plum 151
Child Pose 115–16, *116*, 117
children

and boundaries/rules 93–4
and bullies 102
impatience with 90–1
as 'parents' 88–9
choline 142
chromium 144
clairvoyants 62, 63
clary sage oil 157
comfortable states 38
common sense 27
comparisons, social 77
concentration problems 55
constructive action 26
control, losing 13–14
'Count to 10 technique' 96
crab apple 152
creativity 58
criticism 98–9
'Crown Pull technique' 17, 19,
47–9
cyanocobalamin (vitamin B12)
141–2
L-cysteine 147

dairy foods 129–32
dehydration 127–9
dental fillings 135–6, 137
dentists 135
difficult people 101–5
distraction techniques 71
distress, paying attention to 13
dizziness 112–13
drugs
psychiatric 51
recreational 51–2

electromagnetic fields 138
elm 152
emotional signs of stress 20–2,
68–9
emotions 43, 67
coping with 68–107
boundaries/rules 91–5
contagious moods 99–101
dealing with difficult people
101–5
emotional self-sabotage 81–4
keeping in check 25–6
practical exercises for 70–81
quick fixes for 69
relationships 87–91

unbearable situations 84–7
using anger constructively
95–9
energy levels
and energy vampires 105–7
self-sabotage of 46–7
Environmental Protection Agency
135
environmental stress 138
equilibrium 11–12
see also imbalance
exercises
Belly breathing exercise 111–13
Overload Soother exercise 17,
19, 70
Protective Shield exercise 80–1
Pyramid of Peace exercise 19,
74–6, *75*
Respect exercise 59, 77–80
Screen exercise 49–50, 59
Stress Tap exercise 72–4, *73*
Under-8-Breathing exercise
70–1
Wake-up Call exercises 110–11
exhaustion 40
exercises for 113–14
and glands 159–62
as Phase Three of the stress
response 12
eye contact 102

fainting 112–13
families 88–9, 94–5
fatty acid supplements 146,
147–8
fear
of flying 14–15
of losing control 95
of new technology 21–2
Overload Soother exercise for
70
feverfew 148
fight-or-flight response 12, 15–16
fillings, silver amalgam 135–6,
137
first aid kits *see* holistic first aid
kit
flower remedies 151–4
flying, fear of 14–15
folic acid 142
formaldehyde 126

freezing
bodily 110–11
mental 55
friends 87–8

GABA (gamma-aminobutyric
acid) 146
generalising 82, 84
gentian 152
geranium oil 157
'getting your point across' 61–2,
83
gingko biloba 149
glands, exhausted 159–62
L-glutathione 147
goals 62–3
'good person' concept 93, 94
guilt 85

happy states 38
harmony 11–12
see also imbalance
headaches 113
Heart Protection Study 133
heavy metals 138
see also mercury
help
asking for 83
giving, at all costs 93, 94
herbal remedies 148–50
holistic first aid kit 138–62
amino acids 146–7
aromatherapy oils 154–9
for exhausted glands 159–62
fatty acids 146, 147–8
flower remedies 151–4
herbal remedies 148–50
minerals 143–5
vitamins 140–3
holly 152
Holmes and Rahe's Social
Readjustment Rating Scale
10–11
Honey with oatcakes 118
hops 149
hormones, adrenal (stress) 12,
15–16
hornbeam 152
hot flushes 134
hypericin 150
hypnotherapy 91

hypoglycaemia 125
hyssop oil 157

imbalance 113
  see also equilibrium
impatience, with children 90–1
impatiens 152
inositol 142
insulin 125
insulin growth factor 1 (IGF-1) 130

Journal of the American Medical
  Association 133

kelp 149–50
kinesiologists 139

lactose 129
Lancet (medical journal) 132–3
larch 152
lavender oil 157–8
laws 92
lemon balm oil 158
Life Change Units (LCUs) 10–11
life rhythm, neglecting 121–4
light stress 38
live water 129, 139
lyophilisation 159

McTaggart, Lynne 73, 80
magnesium 144–5
management of stress 162
  case studies 14–15, 17, 19,
    21–2, 24, 61, 90–1, 94–5
  emotional 14–15, 21–2,
    68–107
  mental 19, 43–67
  physical 17, 108–37
mantras 46–7
meat 159
Medical Research Council 132
meditation 45–6
meditative states 37
memory, poor 19, 55
menopausal symptoms 134
mental illness 134
mental overdrive 18, 46–7, 55–7
mental resilience
  strengthening 43–67
    getting your point across
      61–2

improving your work life
    57–60
  mental self-sabotage 51–7
  positivity 62–5
  practical exercises for 45–51
  quick fixes for 44–5
  time management 65–7
mental signs of stress 18–19, 44
mercury poisoning 134–7
metal, heavy 134–7, 138
milk 129–32
mind 43
minerals 134, 143–5
moods 99–101

nausea, management of 17
negativity 64–5, 84
neroli oil 158
nervous system,
    sympathetic/parasympathetic
    16
niacin (vitamin B3) 141
nicotine 119
no, learning to say 61
nutrition 108
  dairy foods 129–32
  for exhausted glands 159
  processed foods 108, 129
  for sleep 118–19
  sugar 124–6
  supplements 132–4, 137,
    138–48
nutritionists 139

obsessive thoughts 24
offal 159
oils
carrier 155
volatile (aromatherapy) 154–9
olive 153
omega-3 fatty acids 147–8
omega-6 fatty acids 148
Onion and tomato salad 118
osteoporosis 129, 131
other people
  advantage takers 93
  angry 96–8
  resisting the demands of 85,
    86–7
  work colleagues 59
overdrive, mental 18, 46–7, 55–7

Overload Soother exercise 17, 19, 70
oxygen supply 47, 111–13

PABA (para-aminobenzoic acid) 142
pain 26
panic 146
pantothenic acid (vitamin B5) 141
parasympathetic nervous system 16
passionflower 150
past experience
  and coping ability 23
  overcoming 20–1, 35–6, 88–91
  and self-blame 82
perceptions of stress 9
personal beliefs 35–6
personality 20, 22
  stress-prone 27–31
physical exercise 108
physical relaxation 26
physical signs of stress 15–17, 109
  see also body support
physiology of stress 12, 15–17
pine 153
pine oil 158
positive effects of stress 162
positivity 62–5
  testing yourself for 64–5
potassium 131
praise 60
present circumstances 23
prevention of stress 5, 133
prioritisation 66
processed foods 108, 129
procrastination 55
prostate cancer 130
Protective Shield exercise 80–1
Pyramid of Peace exercise 19, 74–6, *75*
  circle *75*, 76
  oval 74, *75*
  square *75*, 76
  triangle *75*, 76
pyridoxine (vitamin B6) 141

quantum physics 63–4
questionnaires
  to assess stress quotients 37–44
  to assess stress-prone personalities 27–31

radiation 138
rationality 43
recipes, anti-stress
  Celery and houmous 118–19
  Honey with oatcakes 118
  Onion and tomato salad 118
recognising stress 9–31
reflexology 113–15, *114*
relationships 87–91
relaxation, physical 26
Rescue Remedy 153
resilience to stress 2–3, 25–7
  four inner strengths 25–7
Respect exercise 59, 77–80
response to stress
  Phase One (alarm mode) 12
  Phase Two (resistance reaction) 12
  Phase Three (exhaustion) 12
retinol 140
riboflavin (vitamin B2) 141
rock rose 153
rosemary oil 158–9
rules 91–5

St John's Wort 150
salaries 59
salt intake 129
sarcasm 97–8
Screen exercise 49–50, 59
sedatives
  aromatherapy oils as 156–7, 158
  dietary 118–19
  herbal 149, 150
selenium 145
self blaming 82
self-encouragement 78
self-hypnosis 17, 48–9
self-praise 78–80
self-respect 77–80, 86, 87
self-sabotage
  emotional 81–4
  mental 51–7
  of personal energy 46–7
  physical 119–29
serene states 37
serious stress 39

shirkers 104–5
signs of stress 13–24
  behavioural 22–4
  emotional 20–2, 68–9
  mental 18–19, 44
  physical 15–17, 109
sleep, nutrition for 118–19
smoking 119–21
social comparisons 77
Social Readjustment Rating Scale
  10–11
social support 87–8
solar plexus 113
solitary lifestyles 60
Star of Bethlehem 153
  stress quotient (SQ)
  assessing 37–44
defining 36
Stress Tap exercise 72–4, *73*
stress-prone personalities 27–31
success, anticipation of 50–1
suffering 26
sugar 124–6
support
  at work 59–60
  social 87–8
sweet chestnut 153
sympathetic nervous system 16

therapy 90
thiamine (vitamin B1) 141
Thought Field Therapy (TFT) 72
thymus gland 159, 161–2
thyroid gland 159–61
thyroid-stimulating hormone
  (TSH) 161
thyroxine (T4) 161
time management 65–7
tocopherols 143

unbearable situations, coping
  with 84–7
Under-8-Breathing exercise 70–1

valerian 150

victims 103
violent people 87
vitamins 131, 132–4, 140–3
vitamin A 140
vitamin B complex 140–2
  vitamin B1 (thiamine) 141
  vitamin B2 (riboflavin) 141
  vitamin B3 (niacin) 141
  vitamin B5 (pantothenic acid)
    141
  vitamin B6 (pyridoxine) 141
  vitamin B12 (cyanocobalamin)
    141–2
vitamin C (ascorbic acid) 140,
  142–3
vitamin D 131
vitamin E 143
vitamin K 131

Wake-up Call exercises 110–11
walnut 153–4
warning signs 13–24, 39
  behavioural 22–4
  emotional 20–2, 68–9
  mental 18–19, 44
  physical 15–17, 109
water
  consumption 127–9
  live 129, 139
  quality 128–9
  retention 127
white chestnut 154
willow 154
women, and alcohol
  consumption 53
work, assessing your happiness at
  57–60
work colleagues 59

yoga 115–18, *116*

Zero Point Field 63–4
zinc 145